WHALE

David Holman

Introduction and activities by Lawrence Till

Heinemann Educational,
a division of Heinemann Educational Books Ltd,
Halley Court, Jordan Hill, Oxford OX2 8EJ

OXFORD LONDON EDINBURGH
MADRID ATHENS BOLOGNA PARIS
MELBOURNE SYDNEY AUCKLAND SINGAPORE TOKYO
IBADAN NAIROBI HARARE GABORONE PORTSMOUTH NH (USA)

First published in Great Britain by Methuen Drama, 1989
First published in the *Heinemann Plays* series by Heinemann Educational in
1992

95 10 9 8 7 6 5 4

A catalogue record for this book is available from the British Library on
request.

ISBN 435 23286 X

Caution

Cover design by Keith Pointing
Designed by Jeffery White Creative Associates
Typeset by Taurus Graphics
Printed in England by Clays Ltd, St Ives plc

Acknowledgements
The author and publishers would like to thank Anchorage Daily News/Frank
Spooner Pictures for permission to reproduce the photo on p. 68 and
Shultz/Sipa/Rex Features for permission to reproduce the photo on p. 69.

Contents

To the memory of Fernando Pereira of the Rainbow Warrior. Killed in Auckland Dock, New Zealand, 10 July 1985.

Introduction

Whale dramatises the coming together of the world's major nations with a number of distinctly personal dramas. Global issues and political forces form the background against which many other individual stories are played out. There is a meeting of several worlds: Inuit with American and Russian; ancient with modern; old with young, and mythical with real. The play is a fusion of these to show the closeness of all of them in our lives.

Whale is a chronicle play in that it records actual historical events, and an example of epic theatre in as much as these events were of major importance and are dealt with on a large scale. If performing the play, it is unlikely that you will want a wholly naturalistic setting, especially given the far flung locations – Florida golf-course, Minneapolis house, Californian graveyard etc.

Holman uses a storyteller, which is a device of great antiquity and storytelling is a common Inuit pastime. This allows the author to take short cuts both geographically and dramatically at opportune moments. It is possible to experiment with several ways of playing the storyteller – perhaps, for example, with group chorus work.

The animals were written to be played by actors. The whales in the original production were shaven headed actors on trapeze-harness flying wires who performed ariel ballets throughout the play. The other animals were more simply performed using the minimum of costume or props.

At times the speeches of the Inuit and Russians are given in their own languages. These are always followed by translation into English. If you wish to use the Inuit, some guide to pronunciation is given in the 'Explorations' section which follows the script of the play itself.

There are countless ways of producing *Whale* and as many ways of setting it. The play involves not only dramatic storytelling but can also include celebrations, music, masks and movement. Every production will find its particular solutions, and groups will find diversion and delight in solving the natural problems of staging and costume.

The events in the play

Whale is based on the real events of October 1988. Three young Californian grey whales became trapped in Alaska by the thickening winter ice of the Arctic ocean. They were about 6 to 8 kilometres from open water and finding it increasingly hard to breathe through small and shrinking holes in the ice. With media coverage of their plight, they captured the world's imagination and an international alliance of rescuers was formed.

The US National Guard, the oil industry, environmentalists and the Inuit whalers, who usually hunted whales, all joined in a frantic effort to free the trapped whales. They had two problems: the first was keeping open the ever shrinking breathing holes in the ice so that the whales could stay alive; the second was opening up a passage for them through the thickening ice to the open sea.

Attempts were made to tow an ice-breaking barge to the spot to carve a passage to the sea. When this failed, heavy hammers wielded by helicopters were brought in to smash an escape route. On the ground, rescuers laboured with chainsaws and poles to keep the holes open and cut a channel towards the sea. The three whales were given names – Bonnet, Crossbeak and Bone by the biologists, and, more poetically, Siku (Ice), Putu (Icehole) and K'nik (Snowflake) by the Inuit. The Inuit names are the ones used in the play.

A week after the rescue attempt began, however, K'nik had died from exhaustion and pneumonia and the other two were still separated from the open sea by a deep ice ridge which the helicopter hammers could not smash through.

At this point the US administration asked for help from two Soviet ice-breakers. Within two days these had smashed a way through the ice-ridge and joined up with the US rescuers working their way in the opposite direction. At last, over three weeks after the whales first became trapped, Siku and Putu swam to Mexico and their freedom.

The Inuit

Until the nineteenth century the Inuit (which means 'the people' and preferred to the name Eskimo which means 'eaters of raw flesh') believed that they were the only people on the earth. They live in the Arctic regions of Siberia, Alaska, Canada and Greenland, millions of kilometres of land and sea north of the Arctic Circle. Above this line the days are only a few hours long in the winter while the sun never sets in the summer. Average temperatures in January are approximately –25°C, falling to as much as –40°C. It is above freezing only from June to August.

For hundreds of thousands of years the people lived from only the wild produce of their land. The Arctic is full of animals rich in numbers if not in variety. The sea is full of small sea creatures feeding off micro-organisms attached to the ice. These in turn are food for the fish, whale, dolphin, walrus and seal. The ringed seal is the primary food of the Inuit from the sea; on the land it is the great herds of Caribou, the North American reindeer.

The Inuit hunt with enormous skill and ferocity, and until recently what they killed provided them with everything they needed including food, clothing, shelter, transport and fuel. The Inuit had enormous knowledge of animal behaviour and migra-tions, and had to know their land well.

Myths, legends, beliefs and customs play a vital role in the lives of the Inuit. Songs, stories and ceremonies are very important in everyday life, and all incidents are recorded in song, dance or story. Stories are passed down from generation to generation. The most common subjects are animals, the sun and moon and stars.

In the past the Inuit also relied on dreams and visions to guide them in their hunting. Storytellers with particular spiritual gifts sought help when they needed it by going into a trance. Many stories were concerned with spirits.

One spirit in particular is a woman called Sedna. The myth tells how sea creatures were created when her fingers were cut off by humans and fell into the sea. When her thumbs were cut off the whales of the Arctic were created and this is why they are known as 'children of her thumb'.

To have revenge on the Inuit who caused her such suffering she entangles her creatures in her beautiful hair and does not allow them to go to the surface where they are food for the Inuit. In this way she can bring much suffering to the Inuit. The struggle with ice-breakers and helicopters to rescue the whales is set against a mythical background of attempts to appease Sedna and make her happy, so finally releasing the whales from her kingdom.

Questions and activities

The text of *Whale* is followed by scene-by-scene questions to help classes keep track of the action and characters in the play. These are followed by more lengthy explorations and activities which go more deeply into some of the themes and issues thrown up by the play. There is also a chance to explore Inuit language.

The opportunities for further work arising from the play are endless and the 'Resources' page suggests books, videos and cassettes which can be used for exploring the world of whales, hunting and the Inuit way of life. There is also a list of organisations such as Greenpeace and The Whale Club which can provide specific and up-to-date information.

A glossary at the end of the book explains difficult vocabulary in addition to allusions to people and concepts well known in 1988 but not so well known now, eg 'Nancy' for Nancy Reagan.

Lawrence Till

About the Author

David Holman has written more than 70 works for stage, radio, film and opera which have been performed for or by children. His work has been translated into many languages and has been produced on every continent.

Many of these works have explored environmental questions. These include his most performed play *Drink The Mercury* (1972) about the effects of heavy metal pollution on the fisherman of Minamata in Japan; *Adventure in the Deep* (1973) whose subject is the despoliation of the oceans; *Big Cat, Bad Coat* (1980) and *Solomon and the Big Cat* (1987) which both concern endangered species in Africa; and *Operation Holy Mountain* (1989) on the second coming of the patron Saint of animals, Francis of Assisi.

More recently David Holman has produced a stage adaptation of a story by Nikolai Gogol called *Diary of a Madman* which toured the Soviet Union in 1991 after winning the Sydney Critics Prize. Further stage adaptations include *Billy Budd* (1991) and *Beauty and the Beast* (1992). He has also written a film script, *No Worries*, filmed in Australia.

Other widely performed plays are *No Pasaran* (1976), *The Disappeared* (1979), *Pacemaker* (1980), *No worries* (1984) and *The Small Poppies* (1986).

From David Holman

I was already writing this play about the North Alaska grey whale rescue when news came that the shores of Prince William Sound in Southern Alaska had been devastated by one of the worst oil spills in history. The supertanker **Exxon Valdez** had gone aground and hundreds of thousands of birds, fish and mammals, including whales, were going to die.

Earlier I had met the National Theatre's Artistic Director, Richard Eyre, to talk about plays for children and he was looking for a new work that was 'celebratory'. This prompted me to suggest a play based on the story of Siku and Putu and K'nik, the Grey whales you may remember as Crossbeak, Bonnet and Bone. I had been very impressed by the world-wide concern of children in their rescue and a big theatre offered the chance of producing a large-scale work that could pay proper tribute to that concern.

When the details and pictures came in of what damage and death was being done in Prince William Sound, any sense of celebration for Alaska just vanished. In the course of a few months the small victory of the rescue of two whales was now being overwhelmed by the giant ecological defeat of a major oil spill. And my half-finished 'celebratory' play had become a kind of lie.

The reason *Whale* did get finished is, I suppose, the tremendous interest and concern for Putu, Siku and K'nik among children I continued to meet, a concern that symbolised something that spread much further than the ice of North Alaska – to the whole fate of this planet. The whale rescue had given these children hope that we might, before it is too late, learn a different way of seeing this planet. It may be a very slim chance – Exxon among many others were making it slimmer by the day – but it *is* a chance, and perhaps that is worth celebrating with all its ironies. Perhaps such optimism is best expressed in this prophecy of a Canadian Indian from the Kwakkuit tribe of British Columbia:

'When the Earth has been ravaged and the animals are dying, a tribe of people from all races, creeds and colours will put their faith in deeds, not words, to make the land green again. They will be called 'Warriors of the Rainbow', protectors of the Environment.'

So to all 'Warriors of the Rainbow' – best wishes and I hope very much that you find something to enjoy in this play.

List of Characters

Putu (a Grey whale)
Siku (a Grey whale)
K'nik (a baby Grey)
Storyteller
The Raven
Sedna (The Inuit Spirit of the Sea)
Old Inuit Man
Old Inuit Woman
Other Inuit
Inuit Lover 1
Inuit Lover 2
Arctic Fish
Seals
Sea Lions
Elephant Seals
Walruses
Bowhead and Grey Whales
Dennis the Whaler
Young Bill (son of Dennis)
Joe the Whaler
Polar Bears
Mary Lou McKay (Disc Jockey)
Steve (Producer)
Mrs Sandoval (Wife of Alaskan Oil Executive)
Mrs Kaiser (a keen golfer)
Sal the Golfer
Teddy the Golfer
Bob (a young Alaskan Oil Executive)
Charles (a young Alaskan Oil Executive)
Caddy 1

Caddy 2
National Guard General (voice only)
National Guard Sergeant
National Guard Corporal
Minneapolis Dad
Mum (wife of Minneapolis Dad)
Candy (daughter of Minneapolis Dad)
Minneapolis Kids
Miss Soderstrom (a Marina Owner)
Soviet Sailors
Arctic Birds
Soviet Ship Captain
Soviet Second Officer
Ricky (American Whale Rescuer)
Press Photographer
Australian Journalist
Modern Inuit Kids
Old Inuit (Joe's Grandma)
San Francisco Cemetery Guide
Tourists
Spirit of Charles Scammon (a nineteenth century Whaling Captain)

Act One

Scene One

With strong Inuit drum accompaniment the Storyteller comes forward. Drumming breaks up the introduction.

Storyteller Tavvauvussi sursuit. (Greetings to you young ones.) Greetings young ones from the people of the northern ice. Home of the seal, home of the white bear, home of the whale.

From the very ancient times we have lived together with the whale. We cannot live without the whale, the whale cannot live without us. We are the people of the whale.

But we know that, one morning, we may go down to the edge of the ice and no longer hear the call of the whale because the great ships have killed them all. That is why we bring our story. So that the whale which is in our hearts will live also in yours.

It is a story that begins before there were whales in the sea, before there were seals, before arctic fish swam, before the first white bear prowled the ice floes.

Lights come up on the igloo.

Storyteller When all the world was empty except for an old man and an old woman.

The two Inuit appear. An Old Man and an Old Woman. They are lightly singing a song in Inuktitut.

Sunavinuk?
Arvingunavuguk?
Vugungnai?
ai ai ai ai
Arvingudlunu
Pinasuartaulaarpugungai?
ai . . . ai . . . ai . . . ai.

(What shall we be?
Shall we be whales?
Shall we?
ai ai ai ai
Being whales
We will be hunted, won't we?
ai . . . ai . . . ai . . . ai.)

The Storyteller narrates over the whale song.

Storyteller   They lived all alone on a small island of ice in the middle of the icy sea.

The Old Woman takes a vessel from the igloo and comes slowly forward to the edge of the stage.

Storyteller   One day the old woman came down to the sea to get water.

The Old Woman lies down on the ice while the Old Man goes on singing and working.

Storyteller   Not seeing that across the sea was floating towards her - a feather. A black, black feather. And the feather floated right into her mouth.

Old Woman   Aghhhhhhhhhhhhhhhhhhhhhh.

The Old Man stops singing and looks at her as she runs back to him, holding her stomach.

Old Woman   Ajjigingititausimavunga! (Look what's happened to me!)

As the Old Woman tells the Old Man what has happened to her the Storyteller continues.

Storyteller   Time passed and the old woman's stomach grew bigger and bigger and one day she gave birth – to a raven.

The baby Raven is born, and flies to top of igloo.

Raven   Caaaaaaaaaaaaaaaaaaaawwwwwwwwwwwww.

The Raven is a lively, mischievous but slightly funny figure. He caws continuously. The parents try to get it down and baby it. There is a moment of calm and they cuddle the Raven.

Both Inuit   Ohhhhhhhhhhhhhhhhhhhhhhhh. Unakuluk.

Storyteller	The man and woman loved their baby but it was the most mischievous child that ever came into the world.
Raven	Cawwwwwwwwwwwwwwwwwwwwwwwwwwww.
Storyteller	Sometimes they were in despair.
Raven	Cawwwwwwwwwwwwwwwwwwwwwwww.
Storyteller	One day they had something to do and they shut their baby up for a few moments in their house of ice.

They shut the Raven into the house.

Raven	Cawwwwwwwwwwwwwwwwwwww.
Old Man	Tigusingilaurit nuka piak. (Don't touch anything.)
Storyteller	And please don't you dare touch anything, youngster. And especially don't touch the bladder. Back soon. Rub noses.

The Raven calms and makes to cry.

Both Inuit	Ohhhhhhhhhhhhh.

They leave, supporting each other, so tired with the baby Raven.

Raven	Caaaaaaawwwwwwwwwwwwwwwww.
Storyteller	Since the beginning of time a large bladder had hung from the ceiling. The couple didn't know what was in it, but they knew it should never be touched.
Raven	Caaawwwwwwwwwwwwwww.

And the igloo turns round to show the Raven and the bladder. He is pecking at everything on ground level. Then he looks up and sees the bladder. Looks interested.

Raven	Caaawwwwwwwwwwwww.

He starts to look as though he might peck at it.

Storyteller	Until that moment all the world had been dark. Though nobody knew it, it was because all the light in the world was locked up for safety in the bladder. No, Raven!!!!!!

The Raven pecks at the bladder. Bright lights and harsh sounds flood the stage. Raven looks very confused.

Raven Caaaaaaaaawwwwwwwwww.

Both Inuit rush on.

Both Inuit Aghhhhhhhhhhhhhhhhhhhhhhhhhh.

Raven Caaaaaaaaaaawwwwwwwwwwwwww!!!!!!!!!!!

Storyteller Suddenly the whole world was flooded with light. The old man and the old woman rushed to stop all the precious light escaping.

They do so. The Raven is still screaming and looking sorry for himself. The Old Woman closes the bladder while the Old Man beats the Raven on the bottom. He howls.

Old Man Irnikulualuga! (Look what you've done my child!)

Storyteller Half the light had escaped before the old woman could close the bladder. And that is why, from that moment, the world has had both day – and night.

Back to the original lighting.

Old Man Tulugagulualuk! (You naughty raven!)

Old Woman Aksualuk aniqujaudlutigit ikumak. (You've let out so much light.)

They shake their heads and leave. The Raven starts to cry again. Then calms.

Storyteller The raven grew strong and handsome but naturally he wanted to put his beak into everything. He was so curious. He longed to find out if there was anyone else in the world besides his Mother and Father. So one day he flew away.

The Raven flies.

Storyteller Mile after mile across the snow and the ice. Until –

Music.

A group of Inuit enter with an umiak (boat). All the following should have an element of dance in

the movement. Nose to nose singing in Inuktitut.
Leaving the boat they start playing an Inuit game.
A giant cat's cradle.

The Raven lands some way away from the Inuit.

Raven   Mmmmmmmmmmmmmmmmm.

Inuit   Qiuvit? Qiuvit?
Unaktumingai ai
ai iai iai iai … aii iai iai
Nirijaktuvugungai ai ai ai
ai ai … aiangai … ai iai

(Are you cold? Are you cold?
On hot soup eh?
ai iai iai iai … aii iai iai
We can feast together, can't we?
ai ai … aiangai … ai iai)

The Raven watches them with great interest and
copies their game privately with his claws.

The Raven comes towards them shyly and signs
to them that he would like to join in their game.

Raven   Caaaaaaaaawwwwwwwwwwwwww.

They see him. Stop for a moment. Then turn away.
They are very wary of him and perhaps frightened.

Storyteller   Imagine the terror of the Inuit! A great bird had
flown out of the sky. A frightened black bird.
The Inuit smiled at the Raven but hoped he
would fly away. How could they know that the
Raven was lonely?

Raven   Caaaaaaaaaaaaawwwwwwwwwwwwwwwww.

Disappointed he continues to watch them.

Two of the young men are particularly fond of one
young girl called Sedna. Sedna is having her
beautiful hair combed by her mother. The two
young men are courting Sedna. She detaches
herself coquettishly from her mother. The young
men have become a bit too forward. This brings
her nearer to the Raven.

Storyteller   The girl with the most beautiful hair was called Sedna.

The Raven is very impressed. He falls in love with Sedna.

Raven   Ohhhhhhhhhhhh.

One of the young males comes over and signals to Sedna that he wants to marry her.

First Young Inuit   Uvangaqai? (Me perhaps?)

Sedna   Ivviungituq (No. Not you.)

She shakes her head. He returns to the group. Some laughter. Then the other young man presents himself. He offers to marry her too.

Second Young Inuit   Uvanga kisiani? (Me then?)

Sedna   Aakkuqurtuk. (I don't think so.)

Sedna shakes her head.

The Raven is pleased. It occurs to him that Sedna might accept him. He spruces himself up. Shakes up the feathers on his head. Then strides across the stage. He presents himself to the young Sedna.

Raven   Caw. Caw. Caw. Caw.

Sedna looks nervous. She laughs and looks as if she wants some time to think. The Raven looks happy with this.

Sedna goes back to the group and explains to the two young men who have courted her what has happened.

Storyteller   The young men thought the Raven would steal Sedna from them. They must escape with her.

They nervously come over to the Raven. They whisper and sign to the Raven that he will have an answer in a moment. This is to give them time to make their escape as they fear him now.

The Raven looks satisfied. And he goes a few paces off. He ruffles up his feathers again. He is in good spirits. He is now not looking at them.

The two young men carefully and slowly help

Sedna into the boat. Then swiftly and cautiously all the Inuit lift the boat and flee from the Raven to music.

The Raven continues to ruffle his feathers and preen. Then he looks round for her answer. He sees there is no one there. Looks all around. Lets out a giant and disappointed sound. He is very upset and hurt.

Raven   Caaaaaaaaaaaawwwwwwwwww!!!!!!!!!!!!!!!!

He does a small sad reprise of the cat's cradle game. He would perhaps have accepted just to play with someone.

Storyteller   The Raven looked up and saw Sedna in the far far distance disappearing across the sea. She had given him a gift. Naturally the Raven wanted to repay it. 'Come back beautiful long haired human. Come back!!'

But he then determines to do something. The Raven flies off as music tempo increases.

The two Lovers and Sedna enter with the umiak. The Lovers place Sedna in the umiak and then jump in themselves. They take out the paddles and paddle furiously.

Both Young Inuit   Uimak! Uimak! (Faster! Faster!)

After a while they paddle less vigorously. They have been looking back continuously. Now they feel they are safe. The two young men clasp each other.

Then there is a very loud Raven croak. We should understand this to be the cry of a disappointed Raven rather than a homicidal one. But to the Inuit it sounds terrifying.

Raven   *(off)* Caaaaaaaaaaaawwwwwwwwwwwwwwwwww.

A giant shadow of the Raven appears behind the Inuit.

Storyteller   The young men and Sedna were terrified. How could they know – all the great bird wanted was a friend.

With a cry of terror, they pick up their paddles and start paddling furiously again. But the sounds of the chasing and disappointed Raven get louder. The Inuit are shouting at each other, scared that the Raven is going to catch them.

Both Young Inuit　Uimak! Uimak! (Faster! Faster!)

Then they turn and look at Sedna. (It being she, not they, the Raven chases.)

Both Young Inuit　Sedna!!

Terrified, they grab hold of her to throw her overboard. Sedna screams at them.

Sedna　Taimangillusi! (Please don't do it!)

They grasp her more strongly and force her out of the boat. They grab for their paddles. Sedna turns and swims to the boat. The Lovers are trying to get the umiak moving.

Storyteller　The poor lonely Raven sounded murderous to the escaping Inuit. Only if they threw Sedna from the umiak could they escape death.

Sedna grabs for the boat's side.

Raven　*(off)* Caaawwwwwwwwwwwwwwwwwww.

They bring their paddles down on her hands. She screams but still holds on.

Raven　*(off)* Caaaaaaaaaawwwwwwwwwwwwwwwww!!!!!!!

Storyteller　But Sedna she held on. The young men took their knives and slashed down.

Both Young Inuit　Tuqusiliravit! (Die Sedna!)

Sedna　Aghhhhhhhhhhhhhhhh

Storyteller　And Sedna's bloody fingertips fell into the icy water.

Dancers enter and dance in fish-like movement round the umiak.

Storyteller　Sedna's fingertips spiralled deep deep below the surface of the icy water. And slowly they began to turn into the first fishes in the world. But still Sedna held on.

Raven *(off)* Caaaaaaaaawwwwwwwwwwwwwww.

The Lovers look back behind them and raise their knives again.

Both Young Inuit Tuqutaujuksauvutit uvattinut! (We must kill you Sedna!)

And they plunge the knives downwards again.

Sedna Aghhhhhhhhhhhhhhhhhhhh.

Storyteller And now the bloody second joints of Sedna's fingers fell into the water.

Other dancers enter (or previous dancers, if necessary) and dance round the boat as the seals and sea lions.

Storyteller And slowly slowly these turned into the seals and sea lions of the Arctic seas. But still Sedna hung on to the umiak with what was left of her bloody hands.

Raven *(off)* Caaaaaaaaaaawwwwwwwwww!!!!!!

Both Young Inuit Tuqutaujuksauvutit uvattinut. (You must die Sedna.)

And they slash down with their knives again.

Sedna Aghhhhhhhhhhhhhhhhhhhhhhh.

Storyteller And the bottom joints of Sedna's fingers fell into the sea.

Dancers enter (or previous dancers, if necessary), as elephant seals and walruses.

Storyteller And these fingers turned into the elephant seals and the walruses. Now only Sedna's thumb held her to the umiak.

The Lovers slash down again.

Sedna Aghhhhhhhhhhhhhhhhhhhh.

Dancers (or previous dancers), enter to be the whales.

Storyteller   And Sedna's thumb fell deeper than any finger, down and still down to the bottom of the ocean and there turned into the whales of the Arctic, the Bowhead and the Grey.

And Sedna releases her hands from the boat and, as if drowning, joins up with the dancers.

Storyteller   And Sedna too dropped deep into the ocean where she lives to this day. Sometimes she forgets that the humans caused her injuries and allows the fish and seals and whales to swim to the Inuit to become their food. But sometimes Sedna is so unhappy that she neglects her beautiful hair so it becomes matted and ugly. And then the seals and whales get caught in her hair and they drown.

During this the dancers have taken Sedna out.

Slowly and cautiously some Inuit enter and come towards the umiak.

Storyteller   The umiak was found but the storm that Sedna had caused in cursing the Raven had drowned the two young men. The Inuit found only long streaks of blood on one side and the clawings of finger nails.

The Inuit are worried by what they have found. They pick up the umiak and begin to exit.

The first sound of the whale. They look out to sea, amazed.

An Inuit   Qanuruna nipilik? (What is that sound?)

Storyteller   But looking out to sea they saw first the raven crying for the loss of Sedna and promising some day to make good the harm he had done. Then – for the first time on earth the Inuit heard – the song of the whale.

The sound of the whale as Inuit exit chattering to each other.

Storyteller   And today? The people of the Northern ice still hear the whale calling them.

Scene Two

Sound of whale call continues. On the ice.
Howling wind. Amplified sound of a polar bear.
Enter a polar bear. Roars continue.

Young Bill   (*off*) Dad – you see that!!!

Dennis the Whaler   (*off*) Shhh. If there's an injured whale under the ice the bear will show us where. She likes Bowhead meat as much as we do.

The polar bear starts to move off. A final roar. Then the three hunters come on stage, carrying torches or lanterns. Wind still howling.

Dennis the Whaler   Follow me son. I can hear a Bowhead whale calling somewhere. No more junk food for you. Tonight we eat whale.

And Dennis the Whaler and Young Bill start to follow the polar bear.

Joe the Whaler starts to move to the front of the stage with his light.

Young Bill exits. Dennis the Whaler about to exit.

Dennis the Whaler   Joe?

Joe the Whaler   Be a second.

Dennis the Whaler   What is it? Bowhead?

Joe the Whaler   Probably nothing. You go ahead.

Dennis the Whaler leaves. Joe the Whaler moves another couple of paces forward and speaks to himself.

Joe the Whaler   Under the ice. Seal maybe.

Takes his rifle from his shoulder. Ready to fire. The sound of a whale spout. He jumps back.

Joe the Whaler   Kid, you want to see a whale – there's three. It ain't the whale we want but –

To the whales.

Joe the Whaler   You three should be halfway to Mexico by now.

Bill re-enters. Dennis behind.

Joe the Whaler	Three Greys. They got caught in Sedna's hair and now they're trapped on the ice. Looks like a baby, this one. Like a small snowflake.
Dennis the Whaler	Still five tons of meat each. I'll get the harpoon.
Joe the Whaler	They're Greys!!
Dennis the Whaler	It'd feed the dogs.
Joe the Whaler	It's not our whale. We're Bowhead Inuit.
Dennis the Whaler	Joe, they're gonna die anyways. Hole's hardly big enough for them to breathe now and open sea's way too far for 'em to swim to it under the ice.

To Young Bill.

Dennis the Whaler	These need to breathe maybe every four minutes. From here they'd have to be underwater half an hour to get to open water.

There is the sound of a drum beat. He considers their life expectancy.

Dennis the Whaler	I give 'em coupla days maximum.
Young Bill	Dad, this ice ain't that thick yet. Can't they–
Dennis the Whaler	Greys ain't built to break ice son. That's why they head for Mexico September. October ice and these're finished. Drown. Bowhead – bang. Coupla feet thick ice no problem. Bowhead's got a head. Look there's already blood in the water. With little bitty thin ice to break.
Joe the Whaler	Leave 'em to the polar bears. They smell that blood – aghhhh.
Dennis the Whaler	OK. OK. Let's go find a real whale. I'm hungry.
Joe the Whaler	Might tell that girl from Greenpeace 'bout these three.
Dennis the Whaler	Yea, what's *she* gonna do?

A great joke.

Dennis the Whaler	Come out and break ice for them?

Dennis and Young Bill think this is a tremendous joke. Joe joins in the laughter.

Dennis the Whaler	Yea. Unless Sedna starts combing her hair you

three – Hey, call for the Raven. They say he helps hard luck cases.

The wind comes up and they slowly exit still laughing.

Scene Three

Abrupt and loud music. Freddie Ford's Sea Cruise. *DJ speaks rapidly.*

The Raven enters, curious.

Music continues through the following. DJ speaks rapidly.

Disc Jockey Station WXCL in Barrow, Alaska where it's 15 below and falling. This is rockin' Mary Lou McKay and *The Midnight Hour.* Good Moooooorrrrnning Alaska!!!!! Seen that movie? Freddie Ford's *Sea Cruise.* Playin this for you 'cause with the heavy early ice we got up here on the north coast of Alaska this year ain't nobody going on no sea cruise, less it's on an icebreaker. *The Midnight Hour.* I'll have local news momentarily – after this message.

The Raven is listening and watching.

She plays an ad, for local goods. She turns this down. She looks at a single sheet of paper, very annoyed. Disc Jockey flicks switch.

Disc Jockey Mr Producer Man. Stevie?? Yeah, you behind the glass. What *is* this??

Radio Producer (*off*) That's your local news Mary Lou.

Disc Jockey Steve?

Radio Producer (*off*) It's a slow night.

Disc Jockey Listen when you're the furthest North Disc Jockey in the world you don't expect big news, but three iced-in whales??

The Raven pricks up his ears.

Disc Jockey Didn't nobody get drunk in town tonight? Crash a snowmobile? Wasn't nobody born???

Radio Producer (*off*) Hey. Hey. My own kids gave me that story. They ran into Joe the Whaler in town.

Disc Jockey So let them do the show. Whales get trapped all the time.

Radio Producer (*off*) Not where you can see 'em struggling for air from your window!!

Disc Jockey Steve – real news. I ain't reading this.

Screws up whale newspaper and throws it behind her as the ad finishes. She flicks switch.

Disc Jockey   Little delay on the local news here. Meanwhile–

The Raven moves to pick up the discarded paper. And a new record starts as Producer comes in with some different papers. DJ flicks switch again.

Radio Producer OK!!!! Coupla accidents.

Disc Jockey Be-bop-a-lula.

Radio Producer Drunk drivers.

Disc Jockey Tutti-frutti.

Raven excited at what he is reading.

Radio Producer Fish prices.

Disc Jockey Da-doo-RUN-RUN!!!

Radio Producer Hey come on Mary Lou! I promised my kids.

Disc Jockey Steve, this is rock'n'roll talk radio. I got ten phones here. I want news that's going to get them reelin' and a ringin'. Iced-in whales. Forget it!

The Producer goes and Disc Jockey flicks through pages and then places papers on her console and briefly interrupts record which still plays.

Disc Jockey Local news coming right up.

She goes on listening to the music as the Raven finishes what he is reading. Raven goes over to the console as Disc Jockey is preoccupied with setting up a jingle. Raven takes the traffic reports etc. and slowly screws up each of them and throws them away or eats them. Disc Jockey busy and oblivious. The record finishes.

Disc Jockey And now news from the North Slope tonight.

Jingle. She reaches down for the papers.

Disc Jockey Ugh??

Looks on other side of her.

Disc Jockey Ugh?

The Raven places the whale story in her hand.

Jingle finishes. She looks at the paper she has been given.

Disc Jockey Ugh?

She looks around in panic for the news report. This whale story is all she's got.

She makes the best of it.

Disc Jockey cups mike for a second.

Disc Jockey Steve!!!! I'll kill –

She uncups the mike as jingle finishes.

Disc Jockey Heck of a story right here in Point Barrow for you tonight. Coupla kids of my acquaintance brought it in. Didn't think I'd be interested but it touched my heart and I know it's going to touch yours too. Concerns three Grey whales, yep, that's right, one of them no more than a baby, who should have left for the warm waters of Mexico days ago. Seems they've got a hole about thirty feet across they're breathing through but the ice is closing in fast. They're in bad shape. Kids I mentioned want to know if anyone has any ideas out there 'bout what we could do to help them. – on *The Midnight Hour.* Anyone?

Cups mike.

Disc Jockey No-one.

Immediate start to Beach Boys' Good Vibrations *which should be heard in background for rest of scene.*

Raven	Cawwwwwwwwwwwwwwwwwwwwwwwwwww.
	And Raven dances around the stage.
	Disc Jockey, mad as hell, rips off her cans (headphones).
Disc Jockey	Steve!!!! (*Pause.*) Steve!!! Get in here. Whales?? Listen I know how to get phones ringing. Ya hear that silence Steve? Huh? Hear it? Steve, I been getting phones ringing MY WAY all my damn –
	Sound of phone ringing. Pause. Now two ringing. She hesitates. A third ringing.
Radio Producer	(*off*) Mary Lou, lines one, two and three ringing.
	A drum beat.
Radio Producer	Correction. Four and five.
Disc Jockey	Calling 'bout what?
Radio Producer	(*off*) Add six. Somethin 'bout whales Mary Lou. Correction, seven phones. Baby Grey whales.
Disc Jockey	What??
Disc Jockey	One second please.
	Radio Producer enters holding jacket.
Radio Producer	And eight. Suggestions 'bout how to help 'em, Mary Lou. Remember? Little kids' story – touched your heart.
	More ringing.
	Disc Jockey picks up second phone.
Disc Jockey	Whales? Sure. Anything you want to say Sir? Oh Rosie? Age eight wants to – Right. Put her on, Sir.
Radio Producer	Line nine.
	Disc Jockey listens to two phones.
Disc Jockey	Uhuh. Uhuh. Right. Right.
Radio Producer	Correction Mary Lou. Full house. Listen I think I'm going for a cup of coffee while it's sooooooo silent.
Disc Jockey	You do and – !!

	To phone.
Disc Jockey	No. Sorry.
	Radio Producer puts on jacket.
Radio Producer	Boney Maroney, Peggy Sue, Mary Lou.
Disc Jockey	Jerk!!
	To third phone.
Disc Jockey	Not you Ma'am. Steve!! Ma'am, could you give me a second.
	Another phone.
Disc Jockey	Whales. Sure. One second.
	Another phone.
Disc Jockey	Yep. Whales. Excuse me. Steve!! Steve!!
	Another phone.
Disc Jockey	Excuse me. Right back.
	Shouts to Radio Producer.
Disc Jockey	Steve, get those kids of yours in here.
	Radio Producer exits.
Radio Producer	Coffee.
Disc Jockey	Please. Please. Please. OK?
	Radio Producer reappears. More ringing as the Raven dances.
	Disc Jockey still on phone.
Disc Jockey	You think the Mayor should pay to keep the breathing holes open?
	Cups mike.
Disc Jockey	Steve!!
	Uncups.
Disc Jockey	You're six-years-old and you're listening to *The Midnight Hour*? Well that's a very interesting idea Scott.
	Cupping the mike.
Disc Jockey	I don't believe this!!
	To Producer.

Disc Jockey	I want your kids in here, Joe the Whaler, Greenpeace. Anyone. And now!! Please.

As Radio Producer takes off jacket and nods, she turns to new phone.

Disc Jockey	Yes Ma'am. Do I like whales? Are you kidding.

Up Good Vibrations. Mix in sharp burst of Raven's laughter. Brief blackout continuing the Raven's laughter. He is pretty pleased with his role. Raven noise stops.

Scene Four

Music changes and into the light from the back of the stage painfully walks the sea goddess Sedna. Her stumps of hands are bandaged and covered with blood. She makes an angry sound, annoyed at the Raven's interference. She is centre stage.

Sedna	Puijungitiakpagit tulugak. (Oh no Raven. I haven't forgotten you.)

She gestures to call up the winds and the ice.

Sedna	Anurit kailauristsi!!!! Siku kailaurit!!! (Come winds!!! Come ice!!!)

There is the sound of high Arctic winds. Ice and breaking. The radio voice mixes with the winds.

Radio Voice	Station WKCJ Anchorage Alaska. Hopes for the three Grey whales are fading tonight.

Sedna listens to the ice form.

Radio Voice	Night after night Inuit whalers have been keeping the breathing hole open, amazed at the public's interest coast to coast.

Sedna raises her arms. More ice forms.

Radio Voice	But, as I speak, freezing winds are rapidly closing the breathing hole. The Inuit are cutting fast but the ice is freezing faster. They need a miracle in the next 24 hours and I mean a miracle.

Sedna exits.

Scene Five

Lights up and on a golf course in Florida. A pin flag in the centre of the stage. The eighteenth hole. A young woman, Mrs Sandoval, the wife of an Alaskan oilman, waits front stage. She is plenty mad. Two golfers pass across backstage. Mrs Sandoval has a small airline bag (with Alaska Oil Company printed on side) over her shoulder. She has sunglasses on. Looking up the eighteenth fairway with her back to us. She waits, angry. A jaunty older woman golfer Mrs Kaiser enters in tropical style gear with a driver in one hand and a ball and tee in the other.

Mrs Kaiser speaks to one of the departing golfers Teddy.

Mrs Kaiser	Hi Teddy. Whatya shoot?

To Mrs Sandoval.

Mrs Kaiser	Morning.
Teddy	103.
Mrs Sandoval	Morning.

They have never met before.

Mrs Kaiser speaks to the departing Teddy.

Mrs Kaiser	Attaboy Teddy.

To Mrs Sandoval.

Mrs Kaiser	Florida. Ahhh.

Talking while placing the tee for a practice swing. Away from the eighteenth.

Mrs Kaiser	Sun and golf. Heaven.

Mrs Sandoval is still looking up the fairway and replies without interest.

Mrs Sandoval	Right.
Mrs Kaiser	(*shouts*) Fore.

She waits. Someone is there. She tries a practice swing away from the ball.

Mrs Kaiser	Those poor whales could do with some of this, huh? Melt that ice. (*Shouts.*) Fore!! Oswaldo I'm trying to tee off here!!
	To Mrs Sandoval.
Mrs Kaiser	I got three grandchildren won't leave the TV. Oswaldo! 'What's gonna happen to little K'nik Grandma?' I mean what are ya supposed to say?
	Mrs Sandoval has burst into floods of tears. Surprised pause from Mrs Kaiser as the tears flow.
Mrs Kaiser	What's the matter honey?
	She slowly and tentatively leaves the ball and comes over to Mrs Sandoval.
Mrs Kaiser	Honey, what the – I say something?
	Still tears. Mrs Sandoval shakes her head. Mrs Kaiser looks at Mrs Sandoval's airline bag.
Mrs Kaiser	Alaska Oil Company. You on vacation from Alaska honey?
	A nod with tears.
Mrs Kaiser	What? You upset about those poor whales?
	A nod with tears.
Mrs Kaiser	You've seen them?
	A nod and calming tears. A handkerchief is given.
Mrs Kaiser	Blow. Don't worry about it. I got a million handkerchiefs. Hay fever. Had it all my – Again.
Mrs Sandoval	Flying south pilot took the plane down real low over the ice so we could all–
	Mrs Sandoval bursts into tears again.
Mrs Kaiser	It's OK honey.
Mrs Sandoval	I'm Pisces. I can't help it.
	From the back a woman golfer enters across the eighteenth with her caddy carrying a golf bag. The caddy is the Raven.
Mrs Sandoval	You could see their poor bloodsoaked heads crashing the ice just trying to get air. It isn't

much to ask is it? Air?? But my husband won't
help them get air.

*Raven has of course listened to this with great
interest as he walks.*

Mrs Kaiser   Hus – ?

To the Golfer.

Mrs Kaiser   Hi Sal. Whatya shoot?

Sal   Ninety-six.

Mrs Kaiser   Attagirl.

To Mrs Sandoval.

Mrs Kaiser   Honey those Eskimos are doing all they can.

Mrs Sandoval points up the fairway.

Mrs Sandoval   But Alaska Oil could save those whales if …!!!

A shiver of music. The Raven stops.

Mrs Sandoval   I'm leaving him. My husband is a wimp!!! Wimp!!

Mrs Kaiser   Wait a – Alaska Oil? Your husband works for – ?

Pointing up fairway.

Mrs Kaiser   That him with the other guy?

*The Raven has tapped Sal on the shoulder. Gives
her the golf bag. His caddy instinct is over. Sal is
surprised. Raven pushes her roughly off stage.*

Mrs Sandoval   Those two are sitting on equipment up there
could break that ice. Their boss is away in
Europe. I told Chuck – steal the stuff. Do
something! 'Can't honey.' Everything by the
book. They're not men they're yuppie mouses.

*The Raven stands close now listening attentively
to the two women.*

Mrs Kaiser   Mice.

Drum beat.

Mrs Kaiser   Sorry.

Charles (Mr Sandoval) calls up from the fairway.

Charles   Fore!!!!!

Mrs Sandoval   I married a yuppie mice.

A golf ball arrives.

Mrs Sandoval   A little mice.

Then another ball. Mrs Sandoval indicates her husband's ball.

Mrs Sandoval   He plays golf when he could be – Poor little K'nik!! I'm packed. I'm leaving him.

Mrs Kaiser guides Mrs Sandoval.

Mrs Kaiser   You need a drink. Honey you can't blame your husband for not stealing valuable equipment. Probably worth thousands of dollars.

Mrs Sandoval   Millions. So what?

Resisting being taken.

Mrs Sandoval   No.

Mrs Kaiser   Honey. Someone'll save those whales.

Mrs Sandoval points up fairway.

Mrs Sandoval   Only those two can save 'em. AND THEY WON'T!!!!!

They exit while the Raven quickly comes to a decision. Voices are heard approaching.

Raven   Caaaaaaaaawwwwwwwwwww

He looks up the fairway and then steals both balls. He puts them in his beak. He stands aside as Bob and Charles, the two golfers, enter carrying putters. Their caddies stand at the back silent. Both golfers look extremely puzzled not to see their golf balls.

Bob looks around for his ball.

Bob   Wait a minute. Just wait a minute! I hit the green.

Charles   Me too. I don't believe this. Hey hey. Know what's happened?

Bob   Hole in one!! No.

They rush to the hole with a tiny hope that they have miraculously holed out. Bob pulls out the pin. Cup is empty. They slump.

Bob OK guys let's check the rough.

Caddies start checking back area of stage. The golfers front.

Charles I saw mine hit the green!!!

Bob demonstrates the empty green.

Bob Sure you did Chuck.

And they go to different sides of the stage and bend to search as in the long grass. The Raven comes and whispers to Charles as all four search.

Bob talks to the Caddies

Bob Mine's a 'Curtis Strange' guys.

Raven then stands and tip-toeing goes and puts the two balls in the hole. Golfers and caddies still searching.

Charles Bob?

Bob What?

Charles Those whales.

Bob Chuck! Gimme a break.

Charles Idea.

Bob Your dumb wife's dumb idea and it's a no no. Goddamn grass!!

Charles What do they need?

Bob Where is my ball???

Charles A big crack in the ice.

Bob No.

Charles   And what has Alaskan Oil got at Prudhoe Bay?

Bob It's no, Chuck! One. That ice-breaking barge? – you're talking grand larceny. You're talking Alcatraz.

Charles Not steal – borrow.

Bob Two. It's a million dollars worth of equipment. Three –

Charles They're gonna die.

Bob   So they die. We'd be shining shoes.

Charles   Boss wouldn't have to know.

Bob   Whales die. It's nature Chuck. Don't interfere with nature.

Charles   Inter – ? Nature made golf courses? That ice breaker could be with the whales in 24 hours which is all they've got Bob!!

Bob   Four. You can't get the ice breaker to the whales anyways. Lost ball. What do you say? We'll never find these. We ain't got a 'copter big enough to drag it. Ya need a Sikorski.

They stop searching. Raven puts Bob's ball quietly in hole whilst golfers talk.

Charles   Alaskan National Guard has a Sikorski.

Charles uses his club to demonstrate what will be planned.

Charles   'Copter hooks wires to the barge. Drags the barge to the whales and cracks 'em a path to the sea. Freedom!

Bob   Yea? And you're gonna steal the chopper also? From the Army? You wouldn't see daylight this century. Any century.

To Caddies.

Bob   OK guys, thanks. Lost balls. We're through. What did we say? 25 dollars each.

Bob about to get out his wallet to pay the approaching Caddies.

Charles   Let's risk it.

Bob   Chuck you never took a risk in your life. That's why you're earning a hundred grand a year. You're a yes man. It pays. Don't blow it for some dumb whales.

Raven quickly whispers to Bob.

Bob   Hey. If I'd hit a hole in one I'd have done it with you. 'Kay? Steal the barge, then talk to the

Army. I would. Word of honour.

Charles is unimpressed.

Charles Thanks.

Bob Let's go.

They have both drifted back to the flag on the way out. Raven nudges Charles towards the hole. Charles does a double take at the hole.

Charles looks down the hole.

Charles (*Hoarsely*) Bob?

Bob Gimme a break now.

Charles beckons Bob.

Bob Ugh?

Bob steps towards the hole and looks down also.

Bob Oh wow. Oh WOW!!!!

Reaching down

Bob I don't bel–.

Charles How could –

Bob indicates ball.

Bob My 'Curtis Strange'. Hole in one.

He throws his club into the air.

Pause.

Charles Bob. Just then. You say word of honour?

Bob Hey I didn't –

Charles You did.

Bob You got a witness?

To the Caddies.

Bob There you are guys. There's 25 each. And another 20. Bonus.

To Charles.

Don't mean nothing without a witness buddy.

Charles Oh no. Bob. Oh Bob.

Pause.

First Caddy hands back to Bob the bonus 20.

Bob   Hey, that's your bonus.

First Caddy talks to Charles.

Caddy   You need a witness buddy. You just got one.

Second Caddy hands back his bonus 20.

Caddy 2   You got two.

Bob   Wait a minute. Wait a minute.

First Caddy starts cracking his fingers.

Caddy   Mac – you got stuff'll save them whales and you gonna let 'em die – you can come right now and explain that to my two kids. They been up all night for the TV newsflashes.

Then you come to my house and run it past big Louie.

Bob   Big Lou – ?

Caddy   Walk!

Bob   Hey hey I was only joking guys. Uh? uh? Chuck? Right? But listen uh maybe there ain't a plane. Uh? I mean –

Caddy 2   My sister works at the Airport. She'll get ya' a plane.

Bob is still nervous.

Bob   Great. Great. Well emmmmm. Yea. Right. Right.

Mrs Sandoval enters.

Charles   Honey.

Mrs Sandoval   Chuck I've thought it over. I've called my lawyer and it's D.I.V. –

Charles   Can't talk now sweets. We've got whales to rescue.

Drum beat

Mrs Sandoval   What? What????? You're gonna – Ohhhhh. Clark Kent lives! Ohhh.

She throws herself into his arms. The Raven does a back somersault and then flips into the arms of the Caddies.

Raven Cawwwwwwwwwwwwwwww.

          Blackout.

Scene Six

*Immediate sound of whirring helicopter above
the stage. Snow is falling. We see the wheels of
the 'copter and two ropes coming down. Two
strong spotlights coming from the helicopter
beaming down to two points several feet apart on
the stage. A person with back to the audience
with the coloured table tennis bats of the runway
controller. An Alaskan National Guard Sergeant
in the spotlight is securing a rope which runs from
the helicopter above to the stage (as if stage is the
icebreaking barge). Wears big ear plugs. Towards
back stage an Alaskan National Guard Corporal
with big ear plugs is doing the same with a
second rope.*

*National Guard Sergeant is speaking into a
walkie–talkie and shouts above 'copter engine
noise.*

Nat. Guard Sarg. OK general the barge is secured to your
underframe, Sir. Problem is – this barge is so
heavy if it's stuck to the ice anywhere
underneath even your Sikorski ain't going to
shift it. 'Kay Sir.

*And the noise becomes deafening as the 'copter
tries to get lift into the barge. The snow swirls.
The National Guard Sergeant waves arms as if to
help the 'copter lift. Great noise of metallic strain.
He speaks into walkie-talkie again.*

Nat. Guard Sarg. No General. No. Throttle down. Too much!! Too
much!!

*With a crack one of the ropes breaks. National
Guard NCOs dive for the floor. The other rope
breaks. The 'copter sound lightens to a hum. The
Raven enters. Snow still swirling. Raven looks at*

the broken ropes and up to the 'copter as the National NCOs still have their hands over their heads on the floor and are moaning. Raven jumps up and down in frustration.

National Guard Sergeant rises and speaks into walkie-talkie.

Nat. Guard Sarg.   Sir, we'll be ready to try again in 24 hours. Less if the weather don't get any worse.

A drum beat

Nat. Guard Sarg.   General?

A drum beat

Nat. Guard Sarg.   General?

The National Guard Corporal is clearing the stage of the broken ropes etc.

General   *(off)* Soldier I'm just receiving a phone call.

National Guard Sergeant salutes.

Nat. Guard Sarg.   Sir!

General   *(off)* Know who's calling? Congratulating me on teaming up with the boys at Alaska Oil and asking me, soldier, at precisely what time the National Guard is going to get off its butt and be ready to start breaking ice for them there whales. Seems his TV screen at the White House (you gettin' the picture now son?) is telling him they got 16 hours maximum before their breathing holes freeze over. Now, soldier, maybe YOU want to come and tell the President of the US of A, you need 24 hours!!

National Guard Sergeant speaks into walkie-talkie.

Nat. Guard Sarg.   Twelve Sir. Gimme twelve. Sir? Sir? Ten?

The sound of a disconnected phone.

Nat. Guard Sarg.   Help!!!

And he exits shouting.

Nat. Guard Sarg.   Corporal get your ass in gear. We got whales to save and I mean now!!

Raven gives a giant caw of frustration.

Raven   Caaaaaaawwwwwwwwwwwwwww!!

He gets down on his knees and bangs his head against the ice. A big electronic reverberation from his head hitting ice. The air-strip controller with the table tennis bats throws off her baseball cap. Loosens her hair. She turns. It is Sedna. Lights fade as we hear the growing sound of the howling Arctic wind.

Scene Seven

Suburban house, Minneapolis, Minnesota.

Kids, both boys and girls, enter rowdily in grid-iron football helmets in the colours of the Minnesota Vikings. One has the ball. They tackle and block. Screaming and shouting.

Kids   Minnesota Vikings. Minnesota Vikings. Minnesota Vikings.

Candy, daughter of the house, enters with portable TV.

First Kid   Game time guys.

Candy   Who's gonna wup the New Orleans Saints? Gimme a 'V'.

Kids   V.

Candy   Gimme 'I'.

Kids   I.

Candy   Gimme a 'K'.

Kids   K.

Candy   Gimme another 'I'.

Kids   I.

Candy   Gimme an 'N'.

Kids   N.

Candy   Gimme a 'G'.

Kids	G.
Candy	Gimme an 'S'.
Kids	S.
Candy	What have we got??
Kids	VIKINGS. VIKINGS. VIKINGS.

Mum enters.

Mum Quiettttt!!!!!!

Some Kids Mommm!!!!

Mum Peace!!!

Total silence after bedlam.

Mum I'll say this. I'll say it once. Your Dad's got a first customer for his ice breaking invention. Lady's just arrived.

Mum silences someone before they say a word.

Mum Uh!

A drum beat.

Mum They'll want to talk in here. You want to watch the game in the lounge you do it with the sound off – Uh!

A drum beat.

Mum Till the lady's gone. Don't even breathe loud. Uh!

A drum beat.

Mum I do not put this to you for discussion. This is the way things will be.

She turns with a big smile.

Mum Miss Soderstrom.

Dad and customer enter. Dad kisses his wife.

Minneapolis Dad Hi dear.

Indicates for Miss Soderstrom to come forward to the window.

Minneapolis Dad Miss Soderstrom.

Kid (*whispering*) Boy, Candy, is your Mum always –

He freezes as he sees Mum's look.

They watch the screened ball game. Animated but silent.

Minneapolis Dad shouts to Rick who is outside.

Minneapolis Dad OK Rick, start her up so Miss Soderstrom can see how it works.

Miss Soderstrom Four hundred dollars right?

Minneapolis Dad And we deliver.

Miss Soderstrom Looks good. How many ya made?

Minneapolis Dad Just three. My partner and me are just starting.

The mechanical noise of a drill-like sound starts.

Minneapolis Dad OK as you see lake back of the house is frozen – five, six inches. You got a boat – can't use it. Can't fish, can't take trips. For just four hundred bucks and a can of gas you got ice-free water all winter.

Miss Soderstrom Hey. S'like an egg beater!! A big egg beater.

Minneapolis Dad Right.

Miss Soderstrom It's clearing that ice!!

Minneapolis Dad Why don't you step out and try it for yourself.

Miss Soderstrom nods.

Minneapolis Dad Rick, Miss Soderstrom's comin' out. Show her the controls.

Miss Soderstrom If I like it I'm gonna need all three. I run a marina on Lake Superior.

Miss Soderstrom exits.

Mum comes over to Dad.

Mum All three!!! Your first sale.

Minneapolis Dad Maybe.

Mum You've made a terrific ice melting machine, She's hooked.

And she kisses him and goes.

Minneapolis Dad Come on. First sale. Kids, how's the game goin'?

Candy	We're down seven points.
Minneapolis Dad	To New Orleans?
Candy	They just broke into the game with news of the whales Dad.

The Raven enters.

Dad is still thinking of the sale.

Minneapolis Dad	Uhuh? How they doin'?

All the kids turn their thumbs down.

Minneapolis Dad	Oh.

Raven has a Minnesota Viking helmet under his arm and perhaps their shirt.

He comes to sit with the kids.

Dad looks out of the window as Raven whispers to all the kids.

Minneapolis Dad	Atta girl Miss Soderstrom. Whip up that ice!!

Raven is whispering to all the kids and pointing at the noise of the machine. Candy comes over from the TV and stands with Dad.

Candy	That's a great machine Dad.
Minneapolis Dad	Thanks Candy. Half-time?

Candy shakes head.

Candy	Dad can I put one word in your ear?
Minneapolis Dad	Candy I'm busy. OK?

A drum beat

Minneapolis Dad	Sure.
Candy	Whales Dad.
Minneapolis Dad	Whales?

The kids at the TV all start looking at them.

Candy	The Greys in Alaska, Dad. Army ain't managed to shift the barge out of Prudhoe. Inuit can't cut holes fast enough. They're gonna drown, Dad.
Other Kids	That's right Sir.
First Kid	It was on the news Sir.

Candy	Say they could be dead by tomorrow night Dad.
Minneapolis Dad	Thought you kids were watching the Vikings!!
All Kids	Yes Sir.
Candy	If those Inuit guys had you and your machines, Dad.
The Kids	Right.

Dad fends off the suggestion.

Minneapolis Dad	Hey. Hey. Hey. Hey. OK?? (*Pause*). Dead by tomorrow night?

The Kids nod silently.

Minneapolis Dad	Hey. Hey. Hey. No. No Candy. What the – How'd me and Rick get to Alaska? What are you – Two round trip air-fares? You kiddin' me? I –

The kids go immediately into their pockets for all the money they have.

Minneapolis Dad looks at the small change.

Minneapolis Dad	I mean – that'd get me to the airport at Minneapolis. I'm still a thousand miles away. Think I'm a millionaire or something? I'm a working Joe.

Kids look at him waiting, not accusing.

Minneapolis Dad	Come on. Watch the game!

They turn to do so with one eye on him.

Pause.

Candy	Dad the Christmas trip? How much you save if we all didn't go?
Minneapolis Dad	A grand. Maybe two – I don't know. Hey!
Candy	We want to skip that. Save the money. Right?

She looks round the kids. All nod in turn though it hurts them a little. The last one she looks at doesn't nod.

Candy	Rosie?

A drum beat.

Candy	Rosie?

Rosie nods her head.

Minneapolis Dad　No. OK?

Another Kid　Yes Sir.

They turn back to the game. Dad looks at them. Kids half watch game.

Minneapolis Dad　You know how many hours me and Rick worked this week? Seventy-one. Seventy-one hours. I don't need these looks OK. OK? Some day I'd like to watch a ball game. Know what I mean?? Car isn't near paid for. I got a gas bill I – boy. All I need is – Kids!

Quite a pause as he goes this way and that.

Minneapolis Dad　Candy, move. Grab my weekend bag. Quilted clothes.

Candy runs. Dad moves forward and shouts outside.

Minneapolis Dad　Ricky – leave that. Get all the machines onto the pickup. Miss Soderstrom – sorry Ma'am. Those machines ain't for sale yet. Phone you next week. But if you want to see 'em working thick ice watch National TV tomorrow. North Alaska. OK kids let's go. We got a plane to catch.

They crowd round him as Candy returns with bag.

All Kids　Yeaaaaaa.

Candy　Gimme a 'D'.

Kids　D.

Candy　Gimme an 'A'.

Kids　A.

Candy　Gimme another 'D'.

Kids　D.

Candy　And what have we got??

Kids carry Dad out.

Kids　Daaaaaaaaaaaaaaaad!!

Raven　Cawwwwwwwwwwwwwwww.

Kids Dad! Dad! Dad! Dad!

They exit.

Raven does a somersault and departs in a joyous dance.

Scene Eight

North Slope. Alaska.

Lights up. Sound of the whales ceases.

White stage with three separate breathing holes.

Sound of the strong wind. Snow falling.

Music builds.

The two Inuit whalers Joe and Dennis are cutting at the ice holes.

Dennis the Whaler Joe?

Joe the Whaler What?

Dennis the Whaler indicates a storm approaching.

Dennis the whaler Storm.

Dennis the whaler indicates the whales.

Joe the Whaler Yea. Keep cuttin'. Another few minutes.

Dennis the Whaler Think they're goin' to make it Joe?

Joe the Whaler thinks for a moment.

Joe the Whaler Nope.

They continue to cut.

Dennis the Whaler Know what?

Joe the Whaler What?

Dennis the Whaler The whites. Greenpeace. They given these three names.

Joe the Whaler Why they do that?

Dennis the Whaler I don't know. Big one they see barnacles all over her head. Call her Bonnet.

Joe the Whaler Uhuh.

Dennis the Whaler	Middle one. Got a kinda bent jaw. Crossbeak that one.
Joe the Whaler	Uhuh.
Dennis the Whaler	Little one all bloody from breaking ice with her baby head so her skull's coming through. Call her Bone.
Joe the Whaler	Don't like the look of this wind.
Dennis the Whaler	Me neither. So little Billy says he's gonna give 'em names in our language.
Joe the Whaler	Funny kid.
Dennis the Whaler	Big one he's callin' Putu.
Joe the Whaler	Ice? Yea. Good.
Dennis the Whaler	Middle one – Siku.
Joe the Whaler	Ice hole. Hmm. Hey I know what he's goin' to call the baby. The little snowflake.
Both	K'nik.

Dennis the Whaler points at the gathering storm.

Joe the Whaler	OK Dennis let's take five. Holes are big enough to give 'em air for another hour. Let's go to the shelter.

They run as the storm comes up.

Pause.

Sedna enters

Sedna	K'nik. K'nik. K'nik!!

The three whales breach in turn.

They fill their lungs.

Sedna is near K'nik.

Sedna gestures to K'nik. She is going to keep K'nik.

The three whales fall back to the holes.

The ice covers K'nik's hole.

The wind howls.

Sedna exits.

Joe enters.

He checks the holes. Comes to K'nik's closed hole and shouts.

Joe the Whaler sees the iced over hole.

Joe the Whaler   K'nik!!

Minneapolis Dad and Dennis enter.

Joe the Whaler   We're going to need your machine Mister. Now K'nik.

And all rush to the hole and start to crack at it with their ice cutters.

Joe the Whaler shouts above the wind.

Joe the Whaler   Come on. Put your back into it. We've kept her alive for ten days. Can't let her go now. Come on. Do it for K'nik. Come on! Come on.

The hole is slowly made again. Joe goes down on his knees at the hole.

Joe the Whaler   K'nik!!!! Quick, get your machine Mister.

Minneapolis Dad places the ice twirling machine in the water. It starts to whirl.

Joe the Whaler   Good. Good. Great machine. We'll save her. K'nik! We'll save her. K'nik!

The music builds as before.

We expect all three whales to breach now so positive have been the Inuit. And now all three holes are clear. The rushing sound of the whales about to breach. First Putu breaches, breathes and falls back.

Pause.

Then Siku breaches, breathes and falls back.

Everyone round K'nik's ice hole. Hoping.

Joe the Whaler   K'nik. (*Pause*). Come on K'nik!! (*Pause.*) Come on girl!! Come on!! K'nik!!! K'nik!!!!

Only the sound of the wind. K'nik is dead. Dennis lets out a howl of frustration.

Dennis the Whaler   Sedna just won't let her go.

He throws down his ice cutter.

Joe the Whaler   Tell you what I'm going to do. I'm going to harpoon these two.

Minneapolis Dad   You're what? What??? Joe!! Who's kept them alive for ten days? You Inuit guys. Who cut ice all night every night? Harpoon them?

Joe the Whaler   Mister, your machines are terrific. OK you can keep the holes open. Then what? Come here. What do you see out there?

Minneapolis Dad   Ice. Just ice and then the sea.

Joe the Whaler   Five miles of ice to the sea and more ice every minute. We been cutting new holes for these three to lead them towards the open sea. But the sea's icing up faster than we can get them to new holes. We need an ice-breaker and there's no American ships closer than three hundred miles. Dennis, I say we've done what we can. We harpoon 'em and eat them.

Dennis the Whaler looks at the ice hole.

Minneapolis Dad   No.

A pause.

Dennis the Whaler   I guess.

Minneapolis Dad   Awwwwwwwwwww.

Young Bill   *(off)* Dad! Dad!

Young Bill enters running, out of breath. He sees Joe's intentions.

Young Bill   No Dad!

Dennis the Whaler   What's happening son?

Young Bill is breathless.

Young Bill   Dad. You gotta keep the holes open another 24 hours.

Joe the Whaler   Bill, we've done all we can do. It's finished.

Young Bill is still breathless.

Young Bill   Greenpeace been working round the clock trying to get an icebreaker here.

Joe the Whaler	If there'd been one Greenpeace'd have found it. They got all the US shipping lists. There ain't one that ain't days away.
Young Bill	White House made a special phone call.
Dennis the Whaler	Son, even the President can't produce an icebreaker when there ain't one.
Young Bill	President drew a blank. Right. No US ships.
Dennis the Whaler	So – end of story.
	Young Bill shakes his head.
Young Bill	No. Beginning of story, Dad. He made a second call.
Joe the Whaler	What??? But there's no one. Godammit, who Bill??? Who was the call to??
	Music.
	Spotlight snaps on red flags high above the stage held by female Russian sailors in white. This is the crew of the Soviet icebreaker 'Admiral Makarov'. Immediate singing of The Internationale in Russian.
	(Russian dialogue)
	Then, during the singing a loud cawing and the Raven is revealed, among the Soviet sailors holding a red flag.
Raven	Cawwwwwwwwwwww.
	The Internationale builds. During the singing the two surviving whales breach and breathe. Even higher than before. The Inuit cheer and throw their cutters into the air.
	(Russian dialogue)

(Internationale)
(Arise ye starvelings from your slumbers,
Prise ye criminals of want,
For reasons in revolt now thunders,
And at last ends the age of cant.

Now away with all superstitions,
Servile masses, arise! arise!
We'll change forthwith the old conditions
And spurn the dust to win the prize.
(Chorus:)
Then comrades, come rally,
The last fight let us face –
The International unites the human race.
Then comrades, come rally,
The last fight let us face –
The Internationale unites the human race.

No saviours from on high deliver,
No trust have we in prince or peer;
Our own right hand the chains must shiver,
Chains of hatred, of greed and fear.
Ere the thieves will disgorge their booty,
And to all give a happier lot,
Each at his forge must do his duty
And strike the iron when it's hot.)

(Repeat Chorus.)

The Internationale swells to a conclusion as the
front gauze falls. Lights fade. The Inuit continue
cheering as the front gauze comes down.

Interval.

Act Two

Scene One

Music begins.

Bring up light on stage and we see through front cloth the fog. Cloth taken out and fog covers the stage. In the fog we hear but don't see the whales breach and breathe. Weaker now. They dive.

Out of the fog comes Sedna. Arctic sea birds come to her out of the fog – the creatures of her realm. She is friendly with them. Touches them. They fly off.

Then music changes and through the fog at the opposite side of the stage comes the Raven. His sound at low intense level.

Raven   Cawwwwwwwwww!!

Sedna and the Raven look across the stage at each other as the Storyteller enters.

Raven   Cawwwwwwwwwwwwwwwwww.

Storyteller   'Allow the humans to save these whales, Sedna!' cried the Raven. 'Comb your hair, free them and I promise to fly away and live in some other land. You will never see me again.'

Sedna   (*a strong sound*) Pijjaiunirmat. (Never.)

Storyteller   'Humans? Who cut my hands from me? Who plunder the sea and ice for oil and put all sea creatures in danger? Humans? Who still plunder the sea for the whales, the children of my thumb? Help THEM???

Storyteller starts to move into the fog.

Sedna holds up her bandaged bloody arms to the Raven.

Sedna   Taimak tulugak. Taimak. (No Raven!! No more!!)

The words echo.

The Raven is defiant.

Raven	Cawwwwwwwwwwwwwwwwwwwwwwwwwwwww.

This echoes. Then from behind them a great ripping of ice and creaking iron. The sound of the Soviet ice-breaker. Sedna turns away into the fog. The sound of enthusiastic shouts from the ice-breaker – 'Admiral Makarov'.

Voice off	(Russian)
	(Hello. We're here. The Russians are here. Hello.)

The Raven caws in expectation of success.

Raven	Caaaawwwwwwww!!

The Raven exits into the fog.

Scene Two

Then enter through the thinning fog two female Russian sailors with Soviet flag. These are the Captain of the Soviet icebreaker 'Admiral Makarov' and the ship's 2nd Officer.

Then enter from another direction Minneapolis Dad and his mate Ricky with an American Flag

Then entering from a third direction – two Inuit: Joe and Dennis. They stand watching the meeting.

Soviet Ship Captain	American!!
Minneapolis Dad	Russki! *Perestroika!*

Soviet Ship Captain points at American, friendly.

Soviet Ship Captain	Perry Mason! I – from Georgia.
Minneapolis Dad	What? I was born in Georgia. Atlanta.
Soviet Ship Captain	Tibilisi.

Soviet Ship Captain sings as Ray Charles.

Soviet Ship Captain	Georgia. Georgia.

They laugh and hug. As they do so flags are planted in the ice.

Soviet 2nd Officer	She Captain. Ice break ship. No good English her.

Minneapolis Dad, still close to Soviet Ship Captain, disagrees.

Minneapolis Dad	Fantastic English.
	Sings as Ray Charles.
Minneapolis Dad	Georgia.
Soviet Ship Captain	Siku, Putu good?
	Ricky demonstrates what he says.
Ricky	Not too good. Jagged ice in breathing holes. Hurt heads. Blood. Not so strong now.
	Sound of helicopter.
Minneapolis Dad	Not again!!
	To Russians
Minneapolis Dad	TV. Newspapers.
	Second Officer talks to Captain.
Soviet Ship Captain	(Russian)
	*(*TV. Newspapers.*)*
Soviet Ship Captain	Ah. New York Times. NBC.
Ricky	Toronto Star. El Pais. London Daily Mail. Corriere de la Sera. You can't move around here.
	A rope ladder falls from the top.
Minneapolis Dad	Hey, you guys. These whales are in bad shape now. Media Whirlibirds comin' over on the hour every hour they don't need. So – last picture.
	This as a Photographer has come down a few feet on the rope ladder so he can be seen by everyone.
Photographer	Hey guys, these whales belong to the world now. This is the front page. Not Madonna. Not Nancy. These.
Ricky	Listen pal. When you press guys start cutting ice like these Inuit been doing for two weeks straight – at night, all night – then you can call the shots. Photo finito – comprende?
Photographer	OKKKKKKKKK. OK. buddy. But hey, Russians and Americans working together? That hasn't happened since the war. So ya wanna do the hug one more time? Glasnost right. Mickey Mouse

and the Bear.

They nod and clasp and pose. All looking up at the camera.

Soviet Ship Captain Vodka.

Minneapolis Dad Coca Cola.

Ricky Cheese.

Soviet Ship Captain Cheese?

Soviet 2nd Officer explains.

Soviet 2nd Officer (Russian)

(Smile, please.)

Soviet Ship Captain Ahhh!!

All Cheese.

Photographer Thanks guys. All the best. Set them free.

He is pulled up on the rope as the helicopter noise continues.

Soviet Ship Captain Putu? Siku?

Joe gets out a large map and starts to unfold it.

Minneapolis Dad Behind us. We're keeping away. Give them a bit of peace.

Soviet 2nd Officer explains to Soviet Ship Captain.

Soviet 2nd Officer (Russian)

(They're behind us.)

Soviet Ship Captain (Russian)

(Tell the Americans our specifications.)

Soviet 2nd Officer OK. Strategic. The Captain say you we rip any ice you got so long as we got six metres water under ship.

Joe the Whaler has now spread the map. Map is like an Inuit painting. It shows: the outline of the coast including the Inuit settlement with pictures of the Inuit; the original holes where the whales were found; ice holes leading from there towards the sea; the pack ice and sea channels beyond the ice; in the pack ice the Russian ships; the whales in the furthest ice hole to seaward; polar bears on other patches of ice; a helicopter above the whales with photographers; Inuit cutting the new ice holes.

Joe the Whaler goes swiftly through the map.

Joe the Whaler   Whales originally I find here.

Indicates where.

Joe the Whaler   Inuit been cutting new ice holes for two weeks. Edge of the ice two weeks ago was here. Temperature's dropped 20 degrees and now ice this far out and moving fast.

Simultaneous quiet translation to the Soviet Captain by the Soviet 2nd Officer.

Soviet 2nd Officer   No problem.

Dennis the Whaler indicates as he speaks.

Dennis the Whaler   OK we think it's deep water in as far as here. Start smashing the channel soon as you like. It'll bring you to within thousand metres of the whales. While you're crushing ice we'll cut new ice holes and come towards you. Here, here, here, and so on.

Soviet 2nd Officer   When Siku, Putu reach open sea? Good chance?

Ricky indicates on the map.

Ricky   Latest satellite pictures show there are leads for them to swim in all through the Chukchi sea. They've got every chance of spending Christmas off Mexico.

Soviet Ship Captain has been nodding through this. She's understood it all.

Soviet Ship Captain talks to the whales.

Soviet Ship Captain   Merry Christmas ladies.

Minneapolis Dad   Thanks fellas!!

And the map is folded as–

Soviet Ship Captain   (Russian)

(OK let's cut goddamn ice!!)

Minneapolis Dad   What did the Captain say?

Soviet 2nd Officer	Captain say, 'Let's cut some goddamn ice!'
	The Americans and the Inuit laugh.
Minneapolis Dad	Hey tell her she sounds just like John Wayne.
Soviet 2nd Officer	John Wayne? Hey. The Duke. Red River.
	They laughingly tap each other. Another distant helicopter sound.
Minneapolis Dad	Jeeez!!! More TV. What's happening?
Soviet 2nd Officer	Our town – Vladivostock. We hear about whales Moscow Radio. All the kids. 'Save Siku. Save Putu.' All the time. 'Siku. Putu.'
Minneapolis Dad	Seems like humans are ready to listen to the whales now instead of harpooning them.
Ricky	Yea? Tell Japan. They ain't listening to nobody.
	Soviet Ship Captain speaks in English, like John Wayne.
Soviet Ship Captain	Let's cut some goddamn ice!
	She starts to walk off with John Wayne sideways walk. They laugh and exit as helicopter noise comes up.

Scene Three

A rope ladder descends. An Australian journalist starts coming down the ladder doing her first radio piece on North Slope. Bush hat etc. Not dressed for the climate.

Aussi Journo	Station 2 Triple Z. Sydney, Australia. North Slope, Alaska (*Cold.*) Cripes!! In the distance I see the Russian boat – the 'Admiral Makarov' starting very slowly from the open sea to crack a great mountain of ice that must be in the way of the whales' escape. Working towards them cutting holes in the ice are gangs of men. Must be Inuit I reckon but they don't look like I seen on the old movies. And I don't see igloos either. Must be somewhere else. Hey but there are some of the local kids running towards the helicopter.

Reckon it must be for some traditional Inuit greeting. They won't understand it but I'll give the traditional Aussie greeting.

She is near or at the bottom of the ladder. The Inuit kids enter.

Aussi Journo	G'day kids.
First Inuit Kid	Hey look. Crocodile Dundee's sister!! G'day.
Others	Yea!! G'day.
Aussi Journo	You've heard of Croc–???
Second Inuit Kid	Sure. Video. You know Paul Hogan?
Third Inuit Kid	When's Crocodile Dundee 3 coming out?
Aussi Journo	Hotel. You know what a hotel is?
Third Inuit Kid	Hotel's full. But my Mum's got a room.
Aussi Journo	I'll take it. I read you take payment in stones or somethin'?
Third Inuit Kid	Two hundred dollars a night.
Aussi Journo	What??? Two hundred – What?

Inuit kids look offstage.

Third Inuit Kid	Hey there's another Canadian TV crew landing.

It looks as if they are about to move off in search of more profitable pickings.

Aussi Journo	I'll take the room!
Fourth Inuit Kid	Need someone to take you to the whales?
Aussi Journo	No. Yes. Yes. How long before they're free?
Fourth Inuit Kid	Our Dads are gonna free the whales by tonight. But you're gonna need a snow mobile or you won't see anything. My big brother's got one.
Aussi Journo	Yea. Yea. Yea. How much?
Fourth Inuit Kid	Two hundred a day.
First Inuit Kid	My sister charged TV Italy three hundred.
Aussi Journo	Two hundred. Oh cripes. I'll take it.
Second Inuit Kid	You hungry Miss?
Aussi Journo	I'm starving. Hey but–

Second Inuit Kid	The only restaurant's booked out. Ya want to eat at my sister's hut?
Aussi Journo	Do I have any choice? How much?
Second Inuit Kid	Twenty dollars a plate.
Aussi Journo	OK. OK. Is it traditional Inuit cooking?
Second Inuit Kid	Yea. Inuit Hamburgers.

Aussie Journo speaks as if to the heavens.

Aussi Journo Get me out of here! No take me to the whales. I got to send a story back to Oz.

She then starts to move off.

First Inuit Kid How ya wanna pay? You on an expense account Lady?

Aussi Journo Company cheque OK? You wouldn't have heard of him but I work for a Rupert Murdoch station.

They all whisper to each other.

All Murdoch!!!

Second Inuit kid whispers.

Second Inuit Kid Twentieth-Century Fox. Sky TV.

First Inuit kid whispers to another.

First Inuit Kid Nuts. We shoulda doubled the price!

Aussi Journo   Or I got American Express.

Kids take the card.

All kids American Express?

A drum beat.

As if they've never heard of it all kids chant.

All kids That'll do nicely!!!!

They exit. Music. Lights down.

Scene Four

On the ice. Sound of Arctic wind. Empty stage with two ice holes. One near front stage and one much further back.

Enter Minneapolis Dad and the Soviet 2nd Officer.

They look in the back hole. Then they come forward to the hole at the front of the stage.

Minneapolis Dad looks out front. The direction of the open sea.

Minneapolis Dad   Maybe Siku and Putu already moved to one of the new holes we cut.

Soviet 2nd Officer   All they need now swim under ice – hole to hole – and they got deep channel waiting them.

Minneapolis Dad   They'd be dead without your icebreaker Russki. Dead and buried.

Soviet 2nd Officer   Which hole Putu, Siku in last night?

Minneapolis Dad indicates the one behind.

Minneapolis Dad   That.

Soviet 2nd Officer   OK you me check each hole towards sea.

Minneapolis Dad hears something behind him.

Minneapolis Dad   What's that?

Soviet 2nd Officer   No!

They hear the sound of the whales about to breach behind them.

Minneapolis Dad   They've come back to the same hole!!! Don't they want to get out of here?

The whales breach in the back breathing hole.

Both   Noooooooooooooo.

Soviet 2nd Officer goes towards back hole.

Soviet 2nd Officer   Siku. Putu. You know what out there? Freedom. Why you not want go there dumdums!?

Minneapolis Dad   Maybe they got too used to being round humans.

Soviet 2nd Officer   Go! Go! Go! You die here.

Minneapolis Dad   Shoot!!

Then Ricky enters.

Minneapolis Dad   Bad news here Ricky.

Ricky   I know. Found 'em an hour ago. But don't worry. Had a great idea to move 'em.

Soviet 2nd Officer   What?

Ricky	What'd make you move fast?
Minneapolis Dad	Shark'd do a pretty good job.
Ricky	Close.
	Into radio.
Ricky	OK Control, play the tape when you're ready and big volume.
Soviet 2nd Officer	What is?
Ricky	Public enemy No 1 for the Californian Grey.
	Straightaway and very loud there is the sound of killer whales.
Ricky	Killer whales. This'll get 'em to the sea and pronto.
	They stand by the front hole to which the whales should be moving.
All	Come on. Come on. Come on.
Ricky	Don't you hear them?? These're the guys that can tear your heads off!!
Soviet 2nd Officer	Dumdum whales! Move out!!
Minneapolis Dad	What's wrong with them? Don't you know who that is??
	Ricky speaks into radio.
Ricky	OK. Turn it off. No reaction.
	The sound ceases. They stand there and look at the whales still in the holes. Then at the back Joe the Whaler comes on. He has a stick with him. Joe goes to the ice hole. He kneels down. They turn to look.
Minneapolis Dad	Joe?
	Joe puts hands to his lips. Talks to the whales and then stands and taps one of them on the head. A loud noise and the whales dive. Music.
	Ricky has a sense of excitement and possible success.
Ricky	What's happening?
	Joe moves forward slowly to the second hole

looking down at the ice. He joins the others at the forward (seaward) hole. The sound of the whales approaching. They breach and breathe. All cheer.

Minneapolis Dad   Joe, tell 'em to do the same for ten more holes and they're looking straight at Mexico.

Joe nods. He taps the head of the whales again. They stay there.

Soviet 2nd Officer   Again. Siku. Putu. Come ladies. Please. Joe, again.

Joe taps them again and walks away across front stage. He looks back. The whales stay there.

Minneapolis Dad   Joe, how about we leave them to you? Maybe they don't want us here right now. And Joe, tell 'em every hour they wait those sea channels the Russkis are making are icing back over.

They nod and go. They don't look hopeful now. Joe looks down at the whales.

Joe the Whaler   Why won't you go? There is something we're doing wrong here but I don't know what.

An Old Inuit Woman has entered.

Joe the Whaler   Grandmother you seen the whale hunt all your life. They won't move. What are we doing wrong here? We're running out of time.

Old Inuit   Those the holes you cut up ahead?

Joe the Whaler   Yes. Big holes.

Old Inuit   How deep's the water under those holes?

Joe the Whaler   OK there's deeper water other directions, Grandmother, but we got a problem. We gotta avoid that great mountain of ice up ahead. Our holes only three, four metres maybe to the sea bed.

Old Inuit   Grandson if you want to save these you'd better start thinking like a whale.

The Raven has entered and listens.

Joe the Whaler   OK. Tell me how.

Old Inuit   What's that whale thinking? She's thinking – there's holes in front of me and yea, they're in the direction I got to migrate. Good. But the water's shallow. My head's telling me that. Could get stuck. Could get stuck below the ice and drown. Hey. What about staying where I am? Least there's a hole here. Least I can breathe. And the water's deep. And there's these dumb Inuit sweating for weeks cutting ice for me. Boy I ain't seen that before. Yea. All things considered I'll stay here.

Joe the Whaler   But they'll die.

Old Inuit   She's confused. She thinks you're gonna go on cutting. She don't know in a few days ice'll be so thick you won't be able to cut it. See, youngster, she don't know what November in Alaska is like. No Grey whale ever saw it. They gone south by October or they don't live to pass on the news.

Joe the Whaler   So what are you saying Grandmother?

Old Inuit   I'm saying you got a problem. Seems like Sedna's unhappy again and her hair's maybe gonna drown them. If that's so there's nothing humans can do about it.

A drum beat.

Old Inuit   One man could have. Scamman the American Whaler. Nothin' Captain Charles Scamman didn't know about Greys. Killed enough of 'em. But he knew 'em too. Better than anyone. Yea. But he's been dead and in the ground in California a hundred years. Pity.

She rises.

Old Inuit   Only one thing you can do, youngster. Eat 'em before the polar bears do.

The Old Inuit goes. Joe the Whaler takes a last look at the whales. He shakes his head. Joe the Whaler leaves. Music changes. Slowly and from several directions a number of polar bears approach the holes. The Raven watches and defends.

Raven   Cawwwww.

                 The whales breach and disappear. The bears get
                 closer to the holes and their kill.

Raven   Caaaaaaaaawwwwwwwwwwwwwwwwwwwwww!!!!

                 The bears roar in return. And with a mighty series
                 of croaks the Raven does a Bruce Lee on the
                 bears. They retreat. But clearly not for ever. They
                 are still roaring at the Raven. As lights fade on the
                 frustrated Raven. What to do?

Raven   Cawwwwwwwwwwwwwwwwwwww.

Scene Five

A graveyard in San Francisco, California. Perhaps
only a single gravestone.

A small group of tourists enter preceded by a Tour
Guide with a megaphone.

Tour Guide   Ladies and gentlemen for the last part of our
                 tour of California – the San Francisco Cemetery.
                 The graves of politicians, film stars, and sailors.

                 The tourists wander around taking pictures etc.

Tour Guide   Of special interest today, I guess, as world
                 interest centres on Putu and Siku, is the grave of
                 the whaling Captain who first discovered the
                 Grey whale off this coast in 1846. Charles
                 Scamman.

                 Raven enters.

Tour Guide   From 1846 until the dawn of this century his
                 whaling ships followed the Greys from their
                 winter feeding grounds in Alaska down to Mexico
                 and back again. Killing whales in thousands.

                 Raven squawks angrily at the tourists.

Raven   Caaawwwwwww.

                 Raven knocks on the gravestone as the tourists
                 move back a few steps.

                 Tour Guide is nervous of Raven.

Tour Guide	Ahem. But in the process Captain Scamman came to know more about the Grey whale than any man has ever done. Perhaps if he were alive he could save –
Raven	Cawwwwwwwwwwww!!!!!!

This frightens the tourists. They start to run.

Tour Guide	Back to the bus folks!!!! This here bird seems a little frisky.

To Raven

Tour Guide	Easy Mac!! Easy!!

Raven knocks again hard on the gravestone. Raven caws again at the tourists and frightens the last ones away. Music changes.

The earth starts to move under the gravestone. A hand comes up and then a second holding a bloody wooden harpoon. Then the earth falls back and man in a top hat and nineteenth-century sea clothes rises through the earth. The spirit of the American whaling Captain Scamman stands. He holds the bloody harpoon.

Raven	Caaaaaaaaaaaaawwwwwwwwwwww.
Captain Scamman	Putu? Siku?

The Raven affirms that is the point of his visit.

Captain Scamman	Raven, do you come to mock us, the ghosts of old harpooners who walk these Californian beaches?
Raven	Cawwww.
Captain Scamman	And what we are obliged to look upon? Where once the pods of Grey whales took days and days to pass as they swam between Alaska and Mexico in their hundreds of thousands now we poor ghosts watch ones and twos, small families and know it was we who hunted them to the very edge of extinction. Never thinking. Never asking – where will the killing lead?

The Raven is agitated.

Raven	Caaawwwww.

Captain Scamman   Too late Raven! They are tangled in Sedna's hair. Perhaps she wishes to save them from the harpooners of Japan who still wait; who still slaughter. And who can blame her wanting to keep her children with her after what we have done!!

Raven   Cawwwwwwwwwww.

Raven insistently grabs the Captain.

Captain Scamman   It's too late Raven.

Raven   Cawwwwwwwwwwwwwww.

Captain Scamman takes hold of the Raven. Music. Raven and the Captain are whipped into the air. They fly.

Scene Six

Raven and Captain Scamman are flying high above the stage as the Storyteller enters.

Raven   Caaaaaaaaawwwwwwwwwwwwwwwwwwwwww.

Storyteller   North along the coast of California they flew. Oregon coast now. Following the migration route of the Grey whale. The coast of Washington State and colder now. Across the border of Canada and ever northwards. A journey Captain Scamman had taken so many, many times to kill the Grey whale. Now he would give anything to save them but how? How?

Raven   Caaaaaaaawwwwwwwwww.

Storyteller   Cried the sad raven when he looked down on the frozen North Coast of Alaska, on Siku and Putu and their poor blood covered heads. Saw how Sedna had allowed the wind and the frozen sea to make another mountain of ice to block the whales' pathway to the sea. He looked down and saw the Russian ship helpless and the Inuit throw down their ice cutting knives in despair.

Raven   Caaaaaaaaaaaaaawwwwwwwwwwwwwwwww.

Storyteller	'Sedna cannot forget the loss of her hands and the ruin of her hair. The whales will die. I know it now.' The Raven looked down into the icy waters and he saw the polar bears.
	Polar bears enter.
Storyteller	Saw arctic fish. The elephant seals. The Bowhead whale.
	These animals have entered, dancing. Sedna enters with bandaged hands. She is the focal point of the dance.
Storyteller	And far far below the surface he saw Sedna with her poor tangled neglected hair.
Raven	Caaaaaaaaaaaaaaaaaaaawwwwwwww.
	The dance continues.
Storyteller	And Sedna looked up through the icy water, saw the Raven and then saw the famous whaling Captain who had killed so many of her children.
	A drum beat.
Storyteller	And saw that he would save Siku and Putu if he could. Might the whites change that much?
Sedna	Tamaanipit Scamman? (Scamman is it you?)
Captain Scamman	Yes it is I, Sedna.
Storyteller	And Captain Scamman reached into his pockets and brought out something which he had made so many years ago from the tooth of a whale. It was a comb.
Captain Scamman	Quickly Raven, show Sedna you love her. You always have.
Raven	Caaaaaaaaaawwwwwwwwwwww.
	And the Raven descends into the sea with the comb while Captain Scamman flies above them. Sedna turns and looks at him. The Raven holds up the comb to find out if this offer will be accepted.
Storyteller	Sedna turned from the Raven and saw above her the trapped whales still bravely struggling to reach the air, struggling to live. But very weak

now. Saw Captain Scamman waiting, waiting. Hoping. Hoping. Could she forgive the Raven and man and let the whales swim for Mexico?

A pause and then Sedna turns to the Raven and nods. Music. Raven starts to gently comb her hair. With her hair still being combed we hear the whales being released from her hair and the ice walls crashing. The dancers swirl in time with the continuing sound over which the sounds of home-going whales are prominent. Music has changed to a Mexican theme, a trumpet and guitar-led band. Mixed with whale sounds. Dancing continues. Fog representing the breaking ice comes down starting to mask the dancers.

Front gauze comes down. On the gauze, giant colour underwater film footage of Grey whales in tropical water swimming vigorously as the dance continues to the sounds of Mexico. The lights on the dancers fade leaving only the film of the whales. Then lights come up on the cast so that their wave and bow to the audience is done with the whales still swimming and sounding.

Questions and Activities

1 Keeping Track

Act One: Scene One

1 Why does the playwright use a storyteller in the first scene?

2 What do we find out about Sedna?

3 What does this scene tell you of Ancient Inuit life?

4 How do people react to the behaviour of the Raven in this scene?

5 What sort of game do the Inuit play in this scene?

6 How is the Raven different from the Inuit?

7 What happens to the Raven in this scene? Why are the Inuit frightened of him?

8 How were the whales created?

9 When do seals and whales get caught in Sedna's hair and drown?

10 Recreate the myth in Scene One in a mime circle. One or two people get up and start miming the beginning of the story – then sit down. The next two must add the next part and so on.

Act One: Scene Two

Discuss

1 Who is Young Bill?

2 What does Dennis the Whaler mean by:

'Unless Sedna starts combing her hair you three – Hey, call for the Raven. They say he helps hard luck cases.'

3   a) What do the whalers think of the woman from Greenpeace? b) Why don't the whalers kill the trapped whales? c) What does this scene tell us about grey whales?

4   Why is there a problem for them?

5   What does this scene tell us about modern Inuit life?

6   Improvise a telephone conversation between Joe and the woman from Greenpeace.

Act One: Scene Three

1   What is 'The Midnight Hour'?

2   What does the producer tell the DJ about the whales?

3   What sort of news does the DJ want?

4   Why is the DJ forced to read the story of the whales?

5   Why is the Raven on the side of the whales?

6   What response does the story get from people listening?

7   Why does the producer pretend to be leaving the studio?

8   What arguments do you think the callers to the studio might have made for trying to save the whales? Improvise or write one or two of the conversations which might have taken place.

Act One: Scene Four

1   Where does this scene take place?

2   Why does Sedna have stumps of hands?

3   What does Sedna do in this scene? Why does she do this?

Act One: Scene Five

1 Who are the characters in this scene?

2 What is troubling Mrs Sandoval? Why does she burst into tears?

3 What could Charles and Bob do to help the whales?

4 Why do they refuse to do this?

5 How does the Raven get them to change their minds?

6 What do you think the Raven whispered to them?

7 Several groups of children are mentioned in this scene – whose are they?

8 Why do the caddies return their money?

9 What does Mrs Sandoval want to tell her husband at the end of the scene?

Act One: Scene Six

1 What are the National Guard trying to do?

2 Why do they encounter problems?

3 Who rings the general and what effect does this have on the operation?

4 How does the Raven react to all this?

5 How does this scene create the atmosphere of tension in the play?

Act One: Scene Seven

1 What is Dad's invention?

2 How do the kids try to convince Dad to help in the saving of the whales?

3 How do you think the kids' view of Dad may have changed throughout this scene?

Act One: Scene Eight

1 Dennis and Joe are puzzled by why Greenpeace has named the whales. Why do you think this is?

2 Why do you think Young Bill decided to give them Inuktitut names? What do these names mean?

3 How has Dennis the Whaler's attitude changed towards the whales since Scene Two? Why do you think this might be?

4 What happens to the whales in this scene?

5 What does Dennis mean by 'Sedna just won't let her go'?

6 Why does Joe the Whaler want to harpoon Putu and Siku?

7 By the end of Act One, who is involved in this international rescue?

8 Improvise a phone call where Minneapolis Dad tells his family what's happened so far.

Act Two: Scene One

1 What is the significance of the Arctic Sea Birds?

2 What does the Raven want from Sedna?

3 Why does Sedna refuse to let the humans free the whales?

4 Why does the storyteller appear in this scene?

Act Two: Scene Two

1 What do Minneapolis Dad and the Captain of the Soviet ship find they have in common?

2 How does Ricky feel about the media attention the rescue is attracting?

3 What is meant by 'Mickey Mouse and the Bear'?

4 Why does Ricky say 'Yea? Tell Japan. They ain't listening to nobody.'

5 In these scenes we have the meeting of people from two major nations. What other groups meet in the play?

Act Two: Scene Three

1 What do the Inuit kids offer the Aussie Journo?

2 What does the Aussie Journo expect the Inuit to be like?

3 Write the report the journalist might have sent back to her paper in Australia.

4 Why do you think the writer has included a humorous scene like this just here?

Act Two: Scene Four

1 What stage has the rescue attempt reached at the beginning of this scene?

2 What is Ricky's invention? How is it supposed to work?

3 Why does the writer include the old Inuit Woman at this stage in the story?

4 What reasons does the old woman give for the whales' behaviour?

Act Two: Scene Five

1 Why is this scene set in a San Francisco graveyard?

2 How does the Raven react to the visitors to the graveyard?

3 What does Captain Scamman think the Raven has come to do? Why should he think this?

4 What explanation does Captain Scamman give for the whales' situation?

Act Two: Scene Six

1 Where do the Raven and Scamman travel from and to?

2 What do they see from the air?

3 Why is the comb so important?

4 If Scamman was able to speak to Sedna what would he say?

5 How does Sedna show her forgiveness of the Raven?

6 How do the two stories (ancient and modern Inuit) meet in this scene?

7 What happens at the end of the play?

8 Eskimo prints are often drawn from above looking down – try drawing the Arctic scene which Raven and Captain Scamman flew over in the same way.

9 Take the storyteller out of this scene and write it as dialogue between Scamman, the Raven and Sedna. You should imagine that they all speak English, but include Inuktitut if you can.

10 Imagine that during Scamman's return to earth he is able to give an interview to the press – journalists from all over the world are gathered in the Arctic. Carefully plan the questions you would ask, then think carefully about how he would answer them.

The Whole Play

1 Children play an important part in *Whale*. Look carefully at each point where children are mentioned and describe how much they influence the events of the play.

2 Give an account of the different attempts to save the whales.

3 How important are the following characters helping to save the whales in the play: The Raven, Sedna, The old Inuit woman, Dad, the kids?

4 If you were to write a play with 'green' issues what would you choose as your subject?

5 Describe the reactions of the following people to the struggle of the whales:
(a) The Raven (b) The DJ (c) The Minneapolis kids
(d) Scamman (e) Sedna (f) Mrs Sandoval
(g) Soviet ship Captain

6 Role play interviews by a journalist with Minneapolis Dad, Joe and the old Inuit woman both before and after the freeing of the whales.

7 How do members of the press – from newspapers, radio and TV – come over in the play?

8 How important was press coverage in the fight to save the whales?

9 Write a letter (from yourself) to the North Atlantic Treaty
   Organisation to tell them how worthwhile the saving of the
   whales was.

10 Design a book cover or poster for the play using a picture that
   best illustrates the play.

11 The play shows both old and new aspects of Inuit life. Gather
   together everything in the play you think is traditional about
   Inuit life and everything which is modern.

12 Find out all you can about the Inuit and how they live today.
   Write a short background article on them which a journalist
   following the story of the whales may have written.

2 Activities

Myths

1 The Raven Story at the beginning of *Whale* is a 'creation story'
   typical of the type Inuit traditionally tell. The Raven creates
   day and night by letting the light out of the bladder. Later
   Sedna's story also includes a creation myth – the creation of
   the sea creatures.

   Here is the beginning of a creation story called 'The Origin of
   the Winds'. Continue it on your own or in a group:

   The Origin of the Winds

   *Long ago, when the world was still quite new, there were no
   winds at all, neither the gentle breeze of summer not the fierce
   winter gale. Everything was on the shore and, when snow fell, it
   fell straight to earth instead of blowing and swirling into drifts
   as it does now. At that time, in a village near the mouth of the
   Yukon River, there lived . . .*

2 Act out the story of Sedna The Sea Spirit. There are several
ways you could do this:

(a) Someone in role as Sedna asks others to help retell her
story from when she was young and lived on earth.

(b) i) Recreate the story in ten still pictures. As a group,
choose which ten you want to create then arrange the
scenes one by one and hold them in 'freeze-frame'.
While each scene is presented, one of the group says, in
one line, what it shows.

  ii) Now reduce the number of pictures to three or four you
feel are really essential for telling the story.

  iii) Choose one still to make into a dance drama. Move
silently at first, then add whatever you feel will add to
the dramatic effect – eg music, sound effects, lighting,
costumes and props.

Scenes from the Rescue

Which part of the play does this remind you of?

Which three characters in the play might they be?

Improvise what they might be saying.

Which part of the play does this look like?

What do you think the person in front of the camera is saying?

Language

Inuktitut is an Inuit language. The word Inuktitut means 'the way an Inuk does things', or 'just like an Inuk'. You can add – titut to any word. If you wanted to say 'the way an English person does things' it would be Englishtitut.

Inuktitut is completely different from English. It has very many words and ideas that we do not have.

Read the guide to Inuktitut below, then write down what you think these sentences mean.

a) Nanuq tuttu-siuq-guma-puq

b) Tuttu-mik malik-puq Marcusi

Try to write:

c) Just like a caribou
d) She hunts polar bear
e) A polar bear wants to hunt a killer whale

A guide to Inuktitut

Inuktitut words are sometimes very long. They are built up by putting small pieces in the middle or at the end of a simple word. Here are some simple words:

tuttu   caribou (pronounced tooktoo)
nanuq   polar bear (pronounced nanook)
arlu   killer whale (pronounced arloo)
malik   follow

Here are some infixes – they go in the middle of words:
–siuq–   haunt (pronounced see-ok)
–guma–   want (pronounced gooma)
–ngi–   not (pronounced like the 'ngi' in longing)

Here are some affixes – they go at the end of words:

–titut   just like a (pronounced tea-toot)

–punga   I (pronounced poonga)

–putit   you (pronounced put-it)

–puq   he or she (pronounced pok)

You can use these words to make up sentences. If you use the affix –mik it shows that a word is the object of a sentence.

For example:

Marcusi arlu-mik malik-puq. Marcusi follows a killer whale.

Marcusi-mik arlu malik-puq. A killer whale follows Marcusi.

Or you can make up one long word:

Arlu-siuq-guma-ngi-punga. I don't want to hunt the killer whale.

You can put whole words in any order you like. Just remember that affixes always come after infixes, and that infixes always come after single words.

Answers

1 Nanug tuttu-siuq-guma-puq: The polar bear wants to hunt caribou.

2 Tuttu-mik malik-puq Marcusi: Marcusi follows the caribou.

3 Just like a caribou: Tuttu-titut.

4 She hunts polar bear: Nanug-siuq-puq.

5 A polar bear wants to hunt a killer whale: Nanug arlu-siuq-guma-puq

Why Save the Whales?

Although there was a huge international effort to save the trapped whales, a lot of people questioned whether it was worth so much time, public attention and money. Some of those doubts were expressed in newspaper articles at the time.

Discuss the following questions in your group or as a class and make up your own mind on whether it was all worthwhile or not.

1 Read extracts A and B. What does the writer in A think might happen to the rescued whales? What would the writer in B like the superpowers to do next?

2 How much did the whole operation cost?

The multi-million dollar rescue effort has generated enormous public attention although some cynics wonder whether it is worth saving a couple of creatures which could end as quarry to Japanese harpoons. **A**

Hooray for the joint effort by the United States and the Soviet Union to help natives in Alaska free two whales trapped by Arctic ice. Now might the superpowers turn their attention to Japan, which has told the International Whaling Commission it plans to kill about 300 whales this winter for 'research' purposes? **B**

3 Look at extract C. The writer thinks that bigger and more devastating disasters are being neglected in favour of the whales. Do you agree that the whales got too much coverage and public help and these events too little?

As a spontaneous international expeditionary force gathered for what everyone hoped would be, in the most literal sense, the final breakthrough [to the whales], Nicaragua was counting the cost of hurricane Joan, which tried quite hard to demolish an already devastated country. In the Philippines they mourned the loss of nearly 500 people in a ferry sunk by typhoon Ruby – to name but two fresh disasters which will get only a fraction of the attention devoted to the whales. **C**

4   Read extracts D and E. What do these writers think were the
        reasons governments, oil companies and environmentalists
        were willing to take part in the rescue?

Whatever their motivation, the organizations involved in the   **D**
rescue have reaped invaluable publicity, from the whalers and
government agencies to oil companies and the manu-facturers of
chain saws and ice tractors.

The image of the three whales, cut off from the rest of their species, trapped by the encroaching ice and gasping for breath, awakened deep feelings of compassion and opportunism in their fellow mammals. To environmentalists, the three were wonderful advertisement for the larger purpose of saving the whales from commercial fishing. 'Those three whales are messengers for their kind,' said Campbell Plowden, Whale Campaign coordinator for Greenpeace. To the oil industry, which is seeking to open additional Alaskan lands for exploration, donating equipment and supplies for the rescue effort was a way to demonstrate its famous concern for the environment.   **E**

5   Look at extract F. What does its writer say about the power of
        television? Do you agree that television can affect the way we
        feel about things like this?

6   Why do you think thousands of people phoned TV-am in
        favour of saving the whales?

Why all the megalomedian fuss, complete with interventions by both superpowers, about a couple of crusty-looking whales stuck in an icefield?

The rescue effort has drawn in assorted Eskimos, scientists and troops as well as two helicopter-cranes, a giant Galaxy transport plane, a unique ice-cutter specially taken out of mothballs and two Soviet icebreakers. . . . But a straw poll of viewers by TV-am yesterday on whether the rescue effort is worth the money promptly clogged the switchboard as thousands said Yes and only hundreds said No: public interest made manifest.   **F**

It is television which aroused and intensified our interest in the first place. Because the whales got trapped only yards off the Alaskan coast, they were noticed and in range of TV coverage.

Without the camera there would have been no drama, just as there is, philosophically speaking, no noise in the forest when a tree falls if nobody is there to hear.

7 Finally, look at extract G. How would you answer the question
       put by the writer at the end of it?

The save-the-whales urge runs strong these days. When more than 60   **G**
pilot whales beached on Cape Cod last year, residents plunged into the
surf and tried mightily to push them back. And it was those once fierce
whale hunters, the Soviets, no less, who in 1985 saved 3,000 beluga
whales, sending a music-playing icebreaker to free them from a sudden
arctic freeze. What inspires such efforts?

Resources

Information Books

Alexander, Bryon and Cherry, *Eskimo Boy*, A & C Black

Brody, Hugh, *Living Arctic: Hunters of the Canadian North*, Faber and Faber

Cousteau, Jacques and Paccalet, Yves, *Whales*, WH Allen & Co

Credland, Arthur G, *Whales and Whaling*, Shire Publications

Dobbs, Horace, *The Magic of Dolphins*, Lutterworth Press

Dobbs, Horace, *Tale of Two Dolphins*, Robert Hale

Evans, Peter, *The Natural History of Whales and Dolphins*, C Helm

Forkham, Derek, *Surviving Peoples: Eskimos*, Macdonald Educational

Hoyt, Erich, Orca – *The Whale Called Killer*, Robert Hale

Hoyt, Erich, *The Whale Watcher's Handbook*, Doubleday & Co

Hughes, Jill, *A Closer Look at Eskimos*, Hamish Hamilton Publications

Robert, Wally, *Eskimos*, Collins Publishers

Simon, Noel, *Animal Families: Whales*, J M Dent and Sons Ltd

Smith, J H Greg, *Eskimos – The Inuit and the Arctic*, Wayland Publications

Stidworthy, John and Colville, Jeane, *A Year in the Life of a Whale*, Macdonald

Watson, Lyall, *Whales of the World*, Hutchinson

Williams, Heathcote, *Whale Nation*, Jonathan Cape

Videos and Cassettes

BBC TV Zig Zag, *The Eskimos*, Heritage Books (Video available – 1984 BBC Life and Time of Inuit)

Museum of Mankind Education Service, *The Living Arctic* (video and pack)

Fiction
Melville, Herman, *Moby Dick*, Oxford University Press

Organisations
Cretacean Group
Department of Zoology
South Parks Road
Oxford OX1 3PS

Friends of the Earth
26–28 Underwood Street
London N1 7JQ

Greenpeace
30–31 Islington Green
London N1 8XE

International Centre for Conservation Education
Greenfield House
Guiting Power
Cheltenham
Gloucestershire
GL54 5TZ

International Whaling Commission
The Red House
Station Road
Histon
Cambridge CB4 4NP

Museum of Mankind Education Service
Burlington Gardens
London W1X 2EX

Narwhal Inuit Art Gallery
55 Linden Gardens
London W4 2EH

The Whale Club of the World
PO Box 50
Mansfield
Notts

Whale and Dolphin Conservation Society
20 West Lea Road
Bath
Avon BA1 3RL

Young People's Trust for Endangered Species
95 Woodbridge Road
Guildford
Surrey GU1 4PY

Glossary

American Express charge card, which allows people to buy goods and services immediately and pay for them at the end of the month

Aussie Journo Australian journalist

Bruce Lee martial arts film star

Caribou North American reindeer

Cat's Cradle traditional Inuit game using string, for one or more people

Clark Kent the human form of Superman, the comic-strip and film hero

console panel of switches

coquettishly behaving like a flirt

courting trying to persuade someone to marry you

Crocodile Dundee Australian film starring Paul Hogan

Curtis Strange a make of golf ball

glasnost Russian for 'openness'. Used a lot in the late 1980s to describe the growth of democracy in the Soviet Union

homicidal intending to kill

igloo a traditional dome-shaped snow house

Inuit means 'the people'; but more specifically the name given to people living in the Arctic Cricle

Inuktitut	the language of the Inuit
John Wayne	American actor famous for a large number of cowboy films
junk food	convenience and fast food, often of low nutritional value
Madonna	female American singer
Nancy	Nancy Regan, wife of Ronald Regan, American President (1980-8)
Oz	another name for Australia
Paul Hogan	Australian actor who stars in Crocodile Dundee
Perestroika	Russian for 'reconstruction'. Used a lot in the late 1980s to describe big changes in the economy and society of the Soviet Union
preen	trim feathers with beak to smarten the appearance
Ray Charles	blind American singer
Rupert Murdoch	Australian businessman and international newspaper owner
Sikorski	an American helicopter
spruces himself up	makes himself presentable and handsome
'That'll do nicely!'	catch-phrase of the American Express card, used a lot in 1980s adverts for it
Umiak	an open boat made of skin and wood
Yuppie	Someone who is young, ambitious and in search of money

 OTHER TITLES IN THIS SERIES

Children's Ward   Age 12+

Paul Abbott, John Chambers and Kay Mellor
Granada TV

Six scripts from the popular Granada TV series Children's Ward. The plays trace the fortunes of patients admitted to the children's ward and the relationships between them.

Children's Ward also examines the way the programmes are made, and is an excellent medium for discussing the nature of television drama.

ISBN: 435 23285 1

The Play of The Monster Garden   Age 10+

Diane Samuels

Based on the popular novel by Vivien Alcock, this tells the story of Frankie, daughter of the genetic scientist Professor Stein, and the unexpected results she gets when she cultivates 'jelly' taken from his laboratory. The resulting tale is both funny and thoughtful, raising issues surrounding experimentation, the treatment of living creatures and the nature of friendship.

ISBN: 435 23284 3
(The novel of *The Monster Garden* is also available in New Windmills)